JEREMIAH

FIRE IN HIS BONES

STAN KEY

Published by Warner Press, Inc.
Warner Press and "Warner Press" logo are trademarks of Warner Press Inc.

Jeremiah, Fire in His Bones
Written by Stan Key
Copyright © 2017 Stan Key. All rights reserved.
Cover and layout copyright © 2017 Warner Press Inc.

Requests for information should be sent to:

Warner Press Inc.
2902 Enterprise Drive
P.O. Box 2499
Anderson, IN 46013
www.warnerpress.org

Editor: Karen Rhodes
Cover Design: Curtis Corzine
Layout: Katie Miller
ISBN: 978-1-59317-940-3
Printed in USA

TABLE OF CONTENTS

THE SECOND COMING

Turning and turning in the widening gyre
The falcon cannot hear the falconer;
Things fall apart; the centre cannot hold;
Mere anarchy is loosed upon the world,
The blood-dimmed tide is loosed, and everywhere
The ceremony of innocence is drowned;
The best lack all conviction, while the worst
Are full of passionate intensity.

Surely some revelation is at hand;
Surely the Second Coming is at hand....

—William Butler Yeats
(1919)

INTRODUCTION

The prophet Jeremiah lived and ministered in a time similar to what we face today. Of course, the outward differences between twenty-first century Western culture and that of Israel in the sixth century BC are profound, but at a spiritual level the similarities are striking. Like a magnet, the Book of Jeremiah draws us into its ancient context and then speaks deeply to our souls concerning questions and issues confronting us today. Consider some of the parallels between Jeremiah's day and our own.

THE CULTURE IS COMING APART

The nation of Judah once had been a shining example to the nations of how God can bless and prosper a people who put their trust in the Lord. Her wealth, freedoms, moral integrity, and flourishing arts and culture were the envy of the world. But now Judah was spiraling downward in a morass of cultural confusion and moral decay, and the government was impotent to do anything about it! Politically, economically, culturally, and religiously, the nation no longer had a clear understanding of her identity. Judah was no longer a united body of people who understood her place and purpose in the world. Multiculturalism, religious pluralism, and moral relativism now defined her existence. The moral decay on the inside was as destructive as the military threats on the outside. Sound familiar? Today, as we realize the greatest threats to our existence are internal rather than external, we find ourselves inhabiting a world much like the one in which Jeremiah lived.

THE BARBARIANS ARE AT THE GATES

In the prophet's day, Babylon was a rising superpower, upsetting the status quo with her imperialistic thirst for power and world domination. The nation of Judah must have trembled as she realized how ill-equipped she was to respond to such aggressive and violent expansionism. If you find yourself cringing today at Middle Eastern turmoil, nuclear proliferation, suicide bombings, and public beheadings, then you are living in similar circumstances to those Judah faced some 26 centuries ago.

THE CHURCH IS ASLEEP

Perhaps the greatest source of Jeremiah's consternation was the fact that the institutions that were supposed to protect the people actually were hastening cultural decline. The government was populated with corrupt, incompetent politicians. Worst of all, rather than speaking out about the national crisis, the Temple seemed to be preaching a message of health, wealth, and happiness that put people into a deep spiritual slumber. If you sometimes feel the church today is promoting rather than standing against spiritual decay, then you are living in a world Jeremiah would have understood well.

JEREMIAH'S MINISTRY AND MESSAGE

Jeremiah lived in what was perhaps the most difficult time period Judah had ever experienced. He was both a prophet and a priest (Jeremiah 1:1), called of God to address the crisis surrounding him. His message of wrath and coming judgment was a passionate plea for God's people to repent and turn from their evil ways. God was ready to forgive their sin and heal their land if only they would humble themselves and seek His face. But Jeremiah was ridiculed and persecuted by his contemporaries, and his message was, for the most part, rejected. Little wonder he experienced periods of deep depression and often has been called "the weeping prophet."

The title for this book, *Jeremiah: Fire in His Bones*, is taken from a prayer offered by Jeremiah when he was discouraged and struggling with doubt. Should he continue to preach when no one was listening? Should he soften his message to make it more acceptable? If God was leading him, why was his ministry so unsuccessful? It was while he wrestled with such questions that Jeremiah poured out his soul to God:

> *O LORD, you have deceived me, and I was deceived; you are stronger than I, and you have prevailed. I have become a laughingstock all the day; everyone mocks me. For whenever I speak, I cry out, I shout, "Violence and destruction!" For the word of the LORD has become for me a reproach and derision all day long. If I say, "I will not mention him, or speak any more in his name," there is in my heart as it were a burning fire shut up in my bones, and I am weary with holding it in, and I cannot.* (Jeremiah 20:7–9)

While most of Jeremiah's message is a mournful litany of sin and coming judgment, his occasional outbursts of hope and salvation are among the brightest in all of scripture. As the glittering colors of a diamond are seen best when displayed against black velvet, so the glorious promises of God's amazing grace and redemptive purposes are seen best when displayed against a backdrop of wrath and judgment. Placed right in the middle of the Book of Jeremiah, chapters 30—33 are filled with divine grace and mercy. Often called *The Book of Consolation*, these chapters stand out in stark contrast to the rest of the book. Here, we discover the gospel reality that where sin abounds, grace abounds even more (Romans 5:20). God himself will step into the crisis and create "a new thing on the earth" (Jeremiah 31:22), something no one could have imagined. He will break the yoke of the king of Babylon, restore the fortunes of Israel, and establish a new and everlasting covenant with His people. What's more, He will cause "a righteous Branch to spring up for David" (Jeremiah 33:15–16), a new king who will bring salvation to the people. Although their situation indeed is desperate, God will turn their mourning into joy and their sorrow into gladness. He says, "My people shall be satisfied with my goodness" (Jeremiah 31:13–14).

It is difficult to discern a clear outline and flow of thought in the 52 chapters of this complex book. The order of events does not always follow a chronological sequence. Although some have suggested a haphazard arrangement, a simple progression can be discerned:

CHAPTER(S)	EVENT
1	The call of the prophet
2—29	Because of Judah's sin, judgment is coming
30—33	The Book of Consolation
34—45	Judah does not listen to the prophet's warning and consequently judgment falls
46—51	Judgment also will fall on all the nations
52	Historical appendix: the fall of Jerusalem

Woven into this lengthy narrative are questions and themes of eternal significance, relevant not only for the residents of Judah 2,500 years ago, but also for us today:

- How does one account for depression among God's saints?

- What does divine wrath and judgment look like?

- Can God divorce Himself from the people He married?

- Will God's justice or His mercy ultimately prevail?

- Can human nature be changed?

- How does the New Covenant supersede the Old?

- How does divine sovereignty coexist with human freedom?

- How can a citizen of Jerusalem survive and even thrive in Babylon?

- Does anyone truly understand the depth of deception in the human heart (Jeremiah 17:9–10)?

- What is the difference between knowing *about* God and knowing Him (Jeremiah 9:23–24)?

- How does one discern a true prophet from a false one?

A book that attempted to comment on every chapter and theme of Jeremiah's prophecy would be a long and complex one! This attempt is more modest, focusing on those passages and themes that seem most central to the prophet's core message and most applicable to our world today. Jeremiah's prophetic message was not what people *wanted* to hear, but it was precisely what they *needed* to hear! The same is true today. The words of Jeremiah's ancient prophecy will trouble us, and many who hear them will want to protest. But these words have the power to wake us from our slumber, to heal us and change us, and ultimately to save us. As you read this book, allow Jeremiah's prophetic message to lead you first to repentance and then to revival and reformation.

> *If my people who are called by my name humble themselves, and pray and seek my face and turn from their wicked ways, then I will hear from heaven and will forgive their sin and heal their land.* (2 Chronicles 7:14)

THE CALL

Jeremiah 1:1–19

A few years ago my wife, Katy, talked me into making an appointment with an ear doctor. Although I didn't believe it, she was convinced I was losing my hearing. I was surprised by the doctor's first question: "Do you have trouble hearing your wife?"

I thought he was joking. "Well, *she* thinks I do," I responded. "No, I'm serious," the doctor went on. Pointing to a graph that showed the frequencies of various types of noise, he explained what he meant. "See this line on the graph? A woman's voice falls along that frequency." Pointing to another line, he said, "A man's voice falls along this frequency, like my voice right now. Do you have any problem hearing me?" "No, not at all," I responded. Then the doctor made his point. "When a man begins to lose his hearing, the frequency of a woman's voice typically is the first to go. You *are* experiencing hearing loss and your diminished ability to hear your wife's voice is the first symptom."

I don't know why over time men lose the ability to hear a woman's voice, but I do have an explanation for why most of us find it so difficult to hear the voice of the One who created us. Sin makes us deaf to the God who loves us and wants to reveal His plan for our lives. This spiritual hearing loss helps to explain why the Scriptures often picture God as one who pleads with us to listen. (Emphases below are mine.)

> **Hear**, O Israel: The LORD our God, the LORD is one. You shall love the LORD your God with all your heart and with all your soul and with all your might. (Deuteronomy 6:4–5)

> **Listen** diligently to me, and eat what is good. (Isaiah 55:2)

> He who has ears to hear, let him **hear**. (Matthew 11:15)

> Take care then how you **hear**. (Luke 8:18)

> The sheep **hear** his voice, and he calls his own sheep by name… and the sheep follow him, for they know his voice. (John 10:3–4)

> So faith comes from **hearing**, and hearing through the word of Christ. (Romans 10:17)

The Book of Jeremiah begins with a Voice. God is calling. He is seeking someone who can stand in the gap between a holy God and a sinful nation so judgment and destruction might be averted. God calls out, hoping someone will respond, but is anyone listening? Can anyone hear His Voice? Fortunately, a teenage boy has ears to hear.

THE CALL

Proponents of abortion know how important it is to depersonalize the baby in the womb before they can argue convincingly for terminating a pregnancy. Yet God's plan for Jeremiah's life begins long before he is born. In the womb, God deals with Jeremiah as if he were fully human—a person. Looking at the four main verbs in Jeremiah 1:4–5, we see the basic ingredients of a call:

Now the word of the LORD came to me, saying, "Before I formed
you in the womb I knew you, and before you were born I conse-
crated you; I appointed you a prophet to the nations."

I *formed* you in the womb. Jeremiah is no accident. Neither is his
life simply the result of the plans of his father and mother. God is the
author of Jeremiah's life! Although many may want to assert that life
begins *at* conception, God has a much more radical opinion: *Before*
I formed you in the womb I knew you, He says. In God's eyes, life
begins *before* the sperm joins the egg! God thinks of Jeremiah long
before his parents do. Just as a potter forms wet clay to match the
shape he sees in his head (Jeremiah 18:1–6), so God works to shape
Jeremiah into the form He desires: eye color, height, talents, and
so forth. The Master Potter has a plan and a purpose for Jeremiah's
life long before he is even born. The psalmist describes the origin of
human life in the womb in Psalm 139:13–17:

For you formed my inward parts;
    you knitted me together in my mother's womb.
I praise you, for I am fearfully and wonderfully made.
Wonderful are your works;
    my soul knows it very well.
My frame was not hidden from you,
when I was being made in secret,
    intricately woven in the depths of the earth.
Your eyes saw my unformed substance;
in your book were written, every one of them,
    the days that were formed for me,
    when as yet there was none of them.
How precious to me are your thoughts, O God!
    How vast is the sum of them!

"I *knew* you." As a prophet to the nation of Judah, Jeremiah one day would proclaim how important it is for men and women not just to know *about* God but to *know* Him (see Jeremiah 9:23–24). But here at the beginning of Jeremiah's call, we learn it is much more important that God knows us than it is that we know Him. To be known by God means our being is acknowledged, our opinions are recognized, and our feelings are understood. When we are known, our existence is validated.

"I *consecrated* you." The word consecrated also can be translated sanctified or set apart for holy purposes. In the Bible, we learn that numerous objects are "consecrated"—pots and pans in the Temple, days of the year, cities, priests, and so forth. A pot in the Temple, for example, was considered consecrated (holy, sanctified) not because it was better than other pots or because it had no flaws or defects. Rather, it was holy because it was set apart to be used uniquely for God and His purposes. It was not to be used for common or mundane purposes. The genesis of Jeremiah's call came in the moment he discovered that God had a special plan for his life and already had set him apart for that sacred purpose. "You are not your own, for you were bought with a price. So glorify God in your body" (1 Corinthians 6:19–20).

"I *appointed* you a prophet to the nations." The word appointed indicates that God "gave" Jeremiah to the nations. God loves to give! The gospel reveals God loves the world so much that He gave His only son (John 3:16). So, when Jeremiah discovered God was giving him to the nations, he recognized that God was acting in accord with His most essential nature: self-giving love. Jesus drove home a similar reality when He reminded His disciples, "You did not choose me, but

I chose you and appointed you that you should go and bear fruit" (John 15:16).

Eugene Peterson applies the story of Jeremiah's call to our lives today by reminding us that the truly important things in life happen *before* we are born or even conceived! God "knew me, therefore I am no accident; [He] chose me, therefore I cannot be a zero; [He] gave me, therefore I must not be a consumer."[1]

Although many pretend only saints and spiritual giants have a calling from God, the gospel paints a different picture. If we have ears to hear, we *all* are called to a special, God-ordained purpose. Whether it is to be a prophet to the nations like Jeremiah, or a doctor, lawyer, or schoolteacher, we have been called and set apart for holy purposes. To be deaf and nonresponsive to that call is to live a wasted life.

> God "knew me, therefore I am no accident; [He] chose me, therefore I cannot be a zero; consumer."[He] gave me, therefore I must not be a consumer."

EXCUSES, EXCUSES

One of the surest ways to know whether the voice you hear is from God is in how you respond to what the voice asks you to do. If you think you can handle it, then it is probably *not* the voice of God. But if you throw up your hands in panic and begin to come up with a long list of reasons why this idea is totally preposterous, then maybe, just maybe, you are hearing from God!

Jeremiah's response to God's call is similar to what almost everyone in history has done in a comparable situation: he begins to make excuses: "Ah, Lord GOD! Behold, I do not know how to speak,

---

1. Eugene Peterson, *Run with the Horses* (Downers Grove, IL: InterVarsity Press, 1983), 44.

for I am only a youth" (Jeremiah 1:6). In his mind, God obviously has made a mistake. So, Jeremiah offers two classic excuses he believes disqualify him from the mission God is calling him to fulfill.

1. "I do not know how to speak." Jeremiah doesn't think he has the skills and talents necessary to do what God is asking. He feels unqualified, inadequate. Like Moses (Exodus 4:10) and thousands of others, Jeremiah is ready to ditch God's call because of his fear of public speaking. God doesn't respond to Jeremiah's excuse by commanding him to sign up for Speech 101. He does something much better. He touches Jeremiah's lips and says, "Behold, I have put my words in your mouth" (Jeremiah 1:9). As Jeremiah absorbs and comprehends the message God is giving him, his fear of speaking subsides. When the word of truth burns inside with passionate intensity, the fear of speaking and lack of oratorical skills become irrelevant. A sharp spear needs no polish!

2. "I am only a youth." Jeremiah's second excuse centers on the fact that he is young and inexperienced. To be a prophet to the nations requires a skill set he simply does not have. Jeremiah is a rookie, totally unprepared for such a grand assignment. But once again, God responds with gentle firmness: "Do not say, 'I am only a youth'…Do not be afraid of them, for I am with you to deliver you" (Jeremiah 1:7–8). Trusting in the Lord is the biblical answer to feelings of fear and incompetence.

Many miss God's will for their lives and turn their backs on God's call because, like Jeremiah, they feel inadequate: "I can't speak. I'm too young. I'm too old. I'm just a housewife. I'm only a layman. I don't have a college degree. I don't have the time". The excuses are legion. Yet those who know the Bible story recognize that God never has been in the habit of choosing men and women because of their qualifications and gifts. He purposely chooses those who are weak, poor, and lowly to shame the powerful, the rich, and the mighty "so that no human being might boast in the presence of God" (1 Corinthians 1:26–29). God does not choose Jeremiah because he is qualified. Rather, God qualifies him because he is chosen!

> *God does not choose Jeremiah because he is qualified. Rather, God qualifies him because he is chosen!*

THE PROPHET'S JOB DESCRIPTION

Jeremiah receives his marching orders in verse 10, which many scholars point to as the key verse of the entire book. Note especially the six verbs that outline the prophet's basic job description: "See, I have set you this day over nations and over kingdoms, to *pluck up* and to *break down*, to *destroy* and to *overthrow*, to *build* and to *plant*" (Jeremiah 1:10, emphases mine).

Jeremiah is given authority over not only Judah but also "nations and kingdoms." His task is to proclaim the word of the Lord in two different directions. On the one hand, he is to pronounce God's wrath and judgment on those who persist in their sinful ways. God will *pluck up*, *break down*, *destroy*, and *overthrow* those who refuse to repent and put their trust in Him. On the other hand, Jeremiah is to announce God's mercy and redemptive purposes to those who turn from their sin and put their trust in the Lord. God will *build* and *plant* such people. He will give them a future and a hope.

God explains to His prophet that the bad news of wrath and judgment must precede the good news of peace and salvation. Repentance comes before redemption. Before God can build, He must first break down and destroy; before He can plant, He must pluck up. The fact that four verbs are negative and two are positive seems to indicate that Jeremiah will spend twice as much time talking about sin and judgment as he will spend talking about hope and salvation. The next 52 chapters of the book demonstrate that Jeremiah understood his marching orders well.

JEREMIAH'S PROPHETIC VISION

To obey his calling, however, Jeremiah needs more than ears that hear. He also needs eyes that see. "Jeremiah, what do you see?" (Jeremiah 1:11; also see v 13). God gives His prophet two visions that move him from excuse-making evasion to wholehearted obedience.

The first vision is of an almond branch (Jeremiah 1:11–12). The Lord explains, "I am watching over my word to perform it" (In Hebrew, the word almond sounds like the word for "watching"). This vision is meant to anchor Jeremiah in the reality that the words he preaches are not his words; they are God's. This is God's business. The message Jeremiah is to preach comes from the Lord of the universe, and what God says, He will do! Jeremiah is not the author of the message; he is just the messenger.

The second vision is of a boiling pot facing away from the north (Jeremiah 1:13–16): "Out of the north disaster shall be let loose," Jeremiah says God told him (v 14). Judgment is coming on Jerusalem from the northern kingdom of Babylon. Announcing such disaster will make Jeremiah unpopular. He will be hated by almost everyone. Therefore, Jeremiah is instructed, "Dress yourself for work" (Jeremiah 1:17). This is not going to be an easy assignment, but God is there to help His messenger. He will make Jeremiah like "a fortified city, an iron pillar, and bronze walls" (Jeremiah 1:18).

Although many will fight against him, they ultimately will not prevail. This second vision is meant to reassure Jeremiah that even though he will meet fierce opposition, God will enable him to stand strong and persevere till the very end. "As your days, so shall your strength be" (Deuteronomy 33:25).

These two visions provide Jeremiah with the education he needs for the task ahead. The blossoming almond tree fills him with hope that God indeed will watch over His word, bringing to fruition every promise He ever spoke. The vision of the boiling pot helps Jeremiah to remember this world is a battlefield where a conflict of cosmic proportions is being played out. The battle will be fierce, but God already has equipped His prophet with all he needs to stand strong in the evil day. These two visions will help preserve Jeremiah's sanity and keep him focused on his mission when the world around him is spinning out of control.

BASIC EQUIPMENT FOR THE PROPHETIC TASK

Although young and inexperienced, Jeremiah is given everything he needs for the mission to which he has been called: ears to hear, eyes to see, a mouth to speak, a heart to feel, and courage and faith to obey.

Ears to hear (Jeremiah 1:2, 4, 11, 13). God speaks and yet few seem to hear His voice. What causes such deafness? The answer may surprise you: uncircumcised ears (Jeremiah 6:10). It takes a spiritual work of grace to open ears so we can hear what God is saying. Even as a teenager, Jeremiah has the ability to discern God's voice. In the midst of many voices and callings in his generation, he is able to hear the voice of God.

Eyes to see (Jeremiah 1:11, 13). In the midst of cultural chaos and conflicting signals, Jeremiah is able to see clearly what no one else can: judgment is coming, but those who trust in the Lord will be able to survive and thrive even if they are forced to live as exiles in Babylon.

A mouth to speak (Jeremiah 1:9–10). God supernaturally touches Jeremiah's mouth, giving him spiritual power to speak God's truth. But Jeremiah also is a student of Scripture. He "eats" God's words (Jeremiah 15:16): chewing, savoring, swallowing, and digesting the blessed words of God.

> *Judgment is coming, but those who trust in the Lord will be able to survive and thrive even if they are forced to live as exiles in Babylon.*

A heart to feel (Jeremiah 4:19; 9:1–25). Jeremiah is no dispassionate spectator, watching from a distance as God deals with a rebellious nation. He is a living participant in the drama occurring around him, feeling and experiencing personally all that the other citizens of Jerusalem are feeling and experiencing. Often, he simply sits down and weeps in grief over all that has been lost. Anyone who enjoys preaching judgment and wrath is not a true prophet!

Courage and faith to obey. Jeremiah refuses to allow his fears and feelings of inadequacy to control him. Although he knows full well the cost involved, he steps forward in childlike faith and simply says yes to the call of God.

What about you? Are you equipped for the task God has placed before you? Don't pretend you are not called! God wants all His people to be prophets and prophetesses (Numbers 11:29; Acts 2:17–18; 1 Corinthians 14:1).

1. Describe your thoughts and feelings about the statement, "The truly important things in life happen *before* we are born or even conceived."

2. Are you aware of a call on your life? What is the difference between being "called" and being "driven"?

3. Jeremiah "eats" the Word of God. Discuss what this action means. Does "eating" the Bible describe your method of spending time in God's Word?

4. Jeremiah learns that God chooses to tear down and uproot before He can build and plant. Bad news precedes good news. Repentance comes before salvation. Is this how you received the gospel? Is this how you share it with others?

5. Which part of the basic equipment of a prophet (ears, eyes, mouth, heart, and courage/faith) is weakest in your life?

SPIRITUAL ADULTERY

Jeremiah 2:1—4:4

Early in the twentieth century, the world situation looked bleak. A world war had just ended in which millions of lives had been lost and entire cultures destroyed. A new atheistic and militaristic regime had risen in Russia and many dreamed of exporting the revolution on a global scale. Darwinian evolution was redefining how humans understood their most basic identity. The global economic situation was unstable and many countries were seething in nationalistic desires for revenge and expansionistic visions of empire. Looking at the world around him and the century that stretched before him, an Irishman named William Butler Yeats wrote a poem in 1919 that expressed his angst and consternation. He titled it "The Second Coming."

> *Turning and turning in the widening gyre*
> *The falcon cannot hear the falconer;*
> *Things fall apart; the centre cannot hold;*
> *Mere anarchy is loosed upon the world,*
> *The blood-dimmed tide is loosed, and everywhere*
> *The ceremony of innocence is drowned;*
> *The best lack all conviction, while the worst*
> *Are full of passionate intensity.*
> *Surely some revelation is at hand;*
> *Surely the Second Coming is at hand....*

Jeremiah must have had similar thoughts many centuries earlier as he looked at the world situation of his day. "Things fall apart.... Surely some revelation is at hand."

Few situations are more indicative of things falling apart than when a home is ripped apart because of adultery. For a pastor, no situation is more difficult, more volatile, or has more far-reaching and long-lasting consequences than having to deal with marital infidelity. Such situations test pastoral competence at its deepest levels. Adultery provokes not only great pain and suffering for all those involved but also raises what are perhaps the deepest and most significant questions of human existence.

The real issue in marital infidelity is not sex, although that may be the focus of everyone's attention. The real issue is trust. At the deepest level of the most intimate of all human relationships, a betrayal has occurred. Vows have been broken. Adultery does to a family what treason does to a nation: It destroys the foundation. When vows are broken, the words of Yeats' poem are poignantly appropriate: "Things fall apart...."

The Lord is very interested in the words said during the wedding ceremony. In fact, He fills a role similar to that of the best man. He is the official witness to the covenant being made (Malachi 2:14). If the vows are disregarded, He will want to know why! He holds the partners personally responsible for the promises they are making.

The traditional marriage ceremony has two sets of vows. The first are solemn promises made to God. The pastor looks at the groom (and then later, using the same words, looks at the bride) and asks a series of questions:

Will you have this woman to be your wedded wife; to live together in the holy estate of marriage? Will you love her, comfort her, honor

and keep her, in sickness and in health; and, forsaking all others,
be faithful to her as long as you both shall live?

The proper response to these questions is not "I do" as is so often portrayed in movies and books. The proper response is "I will." The bride and groom engage their wills, making a lifelong commitment to live in accordance with the words of the covenant they are making. This vow is made to God Himself.

Later in the ceremony, the bride and groom face one another and make a second set of promises. But this time the vows they make are to one another:

I, _____, take thee, _____, to be my wedded
wife/husband, to have and to hold from this day forward, for
better for worse, for richer for poorer, in sickness and in health, to
love and to cherish, till death us do part, according to God's holy
ordinance; and thereto I pledge thee my faithfulness.

When adultery occurs, both sets of vows are violated. The promises made to God and to one another are treated as if they are negotiable. Words no longer reflect reality. Promises are broken. People drift from one relationship to another with no cement of commitment to hold them together. Adultery is perhaps the most flagrant illustration of Jeremiah's words, "Truth has perished" (Jeremiah 7:28).

WHEN THE VOW BREAKS

The first sermon Jeremiah preaches (2:1 and following) is a scathing attack on Judah, accusing her of marital unfaithfulness. Years earlier, at Mount Sinai, God and Israel had established a covenant together; they got married (see Exodus 19:4–8; 24:3–8; Jeremiah 31:31–32).

God has been faithful to His side of the covenant but Judah has a long history of adulterous relationships. Jeremiah wants Judah to understand that God is experiencing the same range of emotions that all jilted lovers feel when they discover they have been betrayed: grief, hurt, shock, and rage.

Called in to mediate the situation, Jeremiah finds himself standing between a wayward wife (Judah), who refuses to admit her wrongdoing or give up her illicit lovers, and a grief-stricken husband (God), who can't quite decide whether He wants to divorce or to reconcile. Never has anyone had a more difficult pastoral challenge!

The sermon in which Jeremiah addresses this volatile situation begins in Jeremiah 2:1 and stretches as far as 4:4. It has three basic points:

1. God *remembers*: How wonderful were their first days together! It was like a perpetual honeymoon. (2:1–3)

2. *God wants answers*: So why did Judah run off with other lovers? What did He do to offend her and cause her to seek satisfaction elsewhere? (2:4—3:5)

3. *God pleads*: He begs Judah to come home again! He still loves her and is ready to forgive and reconcile. Furthermore, He can heal her backsliding. (3:6—4:4)

Most of Jeremiah's sermon is a recitation of God's own words concerning what has happened. Judah needs to *feel* the consequences of her brazen behavior. Like an offended spouse, God is upset and needs some time and space to work out His emotions. Quoting portions of this sermon from the more contemporary *New Living Translation* helps to drive home the emotional drama of the situation:

*The LORD gave me another message. He said, "Go and
shout this message to Jerusalem. This is what the LORD says:*

*"I remember how eager you were to please me
    as a young bride long ago,
how you loved me and followed me
    even through the barren wilderness.
In those days Israel was holy to the LORD,
    the first of his children.
All who harmed his people were declared guilty,
    and disaster fell on them.
    I, the LORD, have spoken!"*

*Listen to the word of the LORD, people of Jacob—all you
families of Israel! This is what the LORD says:*

*"What did your ancestors find wrong with me
    that led them to stray so far from me?
They worshiped worthless idols,
    only to become worthless themselves.* (2:1–5 NLT)

*Therefore, I will bring my case against you,"
    says the LORD.
"I will even bring charges against your children's children
    in the years to come.*

*"Go west and look in the land of Cyprus;
    go east and search through the land of Kedar.
Has anyone ever heard of anything
    as strange as this?
Has any nation ever traded its gods for new ones,
    even though they are not gods at all?*

29

JEREMIAH

Yet my people have exchanged their glorious God
    for worthless idols!
The heavens are shocked at such a thing
    and shrink back in horror and dismay,"
    says the LORD.
"For my people have done two evil things:
They have abandoned me—
    the fountain of living water.
And they have dug for themselves cracked cisterns
    that can hold no water at all! (2:9–13 NLT)

"You say, 'That's not true!
    I haven't worshiped the images of Baal!'
But how can you say that?
    Go and look in any valley in the land!
Face the awful sins you have done.
    You are like a restless female camel
    desperately searching for a mate.
You are like a wild donkey,
    sniffing the wind at mating time.
Who can restrain her lust?
    Those who desire her don't need to search,
    for she goes running to them! (2:23–24 NLT)

"If a man divorces a woman
    and she goes and marries someone else,
he will not take her back again,
    for that would surely corrupt the land.
But you have prostituted yourself with many lovers,
    so why are you trying to come back to me?"
    says the LORD.
"Look at the shrines on every hilltop.

Is there any place you have not been defiled
by your adultery with other gods?
You sit like a prostitute beside the road waiting for a customer.
You sit alone like a nomad in the desert.
You have polluted the land with your prostitution
and your wickedness.
That's why even the spring rains have failed.
For you are a brazen prostitute and completely shameless."
(3:1–3 NLT)

AN UGLY PICTURE

In preaching this sermon, Jeremiah wants his listeners to understand that spiritual adultery is no minor aberration that can be repaired easily. Being untrue to covenant vows, whether made to a spouse or to God, is a particularly destructive sin.

It is an *ugly* sin. While adultery may be called "an affair," glamourized by Hollywood and portrayed as something beautiful, exciting, and fun, nothing could be further from the truth. "A restless female camel desperately searching for a mate…a wild donkey, sniffing the wind at mating time" (2:23–24) is a much more realistic depiction of what is really happening! There is nothing pretty about backstabbers, liars, cheaters, betrayers, and traitors. Nothing is more hurtful to everyone involved than when a spouse betrays the marriage covenant and begins an illicit relationship with someone else. The damage done to children, families, communities, and nations is incalculable.

The picture becomes even uglier when one realizes that the un-faithful partner is not experiencing a momentary lapse of judgment or has perhaps been caught in some seductive trap. One-night stands are relatively "easy" to repair when the guilty party is repentant and wants to do whatever it takes to restore the marital relationship. But when the offending person brazenly makes repeated choices to turn away from his or her spouse in ongoing, long-term relationships with multiple lovers, it is a truly desperate situation. In such cases, any hope for reconciliation is slim indeed.

It is a *progressive* sin. No one says, "I want to become an adulterer!" Marital unfaithfulness typically begins with "innocent" steps: a look of the eye, a touch of the hand, a tone in the voice. Then, at some point, a line is crossed and the person is on a slippery slope, trapped in cycles of behavior he or she can't control. There *is* a point of no return—and once that point is crossed, the outcome leads inexorably to destruction.

It is a *stupid* sin. Like drinking salt water, adultery simply is not a smart thing to do. It doesn't satisfy; it only makes one thirstier! Adultery is doubly dumb: it causes one to forsake the only fountain of water that satisfies, to construct a cistern that can't hold water at all (2:13). Adultery is the surest way possible to damage children, destroy finances, rupture relationships, and cause regrets for the rest of one's life! Adultery is the pursuit of "worthlessness"—vanity, emptiness (2:5). Once you reach your goal, you discover you have become what you sought: worthless. Is this a goal anyone really wants to reach?

It is a *numbing* sin. In the beginning, adulterers feel guilt over what is happening. They know it is wrong and that it will end badly. And yet, over time, they become habituated to sin. Living in denial, adulterers eventually reach the point where they actually believe what they are doing is okay: "I'm not unclean" (2:23), "I am innocent...

I have not sinned" (2:35). Eventually adulterers' consciences are so dead that they lose the ability even to blush (6:15). When such numbness to sin is widespread in a culture, things fall apart. The barbarians are at the gates.

It is a *serious* sin. Adultery destroys relationships, ruptures covenants, and separates what God has joined together. The wage of adultery is death. "You adulterous people! Do you not know that friendship with the world is enmity with God? Therefore whoever wishes to be a friend of the world makes himself an enemy of God" (James 4:4). Judah's sin was not a momentary lack of judgment. The people of God made a willful and conscious choice to live a double life, pretending to belong to God while at the same time consorting with multiple lovers. The Bible has a technical term for such behavior. Depending on the translation, it may be called backsliding, apostasy, or faithlessness (Jeremiah 2:19; 3:22; 5:6; 14:7; 15:6). People guilty of this sin go "backward and not forward" (Jeremiah 7:24). When such backsliding becomes "perpetual" (Jeremiah 8:5), apart from a miracle of sovereign grace, the end results can be only wrath and judgment.

Adultery is *grounds for divorce* (Deuteronomy 24:1–4; Matthew 19:3–9). Jeremiah acknowledges that God has already "divorced" the 10 northern tribes of Israel (3:6–10) and because of Judah's brazen and continual adulteries, He is almost ready to divorce her as well. He has grounds! And yet, although divorce is permitted, it is not mandatory. If the offending spouse gets rid of the other lovers and genuinely repents, then forgiveness becomes possible, and the marriage might be saved.

Jeremiah's sermon leaves the listeners uncertain about what will happen next. What will God do? Will He divorce Judah? Or will He find a way to bring her home and restore the marriage? It seems as if the outcome rests in the hands of those who are hearing the sermon!

Can the Marriage Be Saved?

Although Jeremiah's sermon at times seems to imply that the marriage between God and Judah is irretrievably broken, it contains numerous promises of hope. God is pleading with His wayward people: "Come home, oh, come home; before it is too late."

> "Return, faithless Israel," declares the LORD.
> "I will not look on you in anger, for I am merciful," declares the LORD;
> "I will not be angry forever. Only acknowledge your guilt, that you rebelled against the LORD your God and scattered your favors
> among foreigners under every green tree, and that you have not obeyed my voice," declares the LORD.
> "Return, O faithless children," declares the LORD;
> "For I am your master." (3:12–14)

Perhaps the most succinct statement of God's love and readiness to forgive is found in Jeremiah 3:22: "Return, O faithless sons; I will heal your faithlessness." The New International Version renders the words, "I will cure you of backsliding."

There is hope. The marriage can be saved! "Where sin increased, grace abounded all the more" (Romans 5:20). No situation is beyond the power of God's redeeming love. Jeremiah 3:22 reminds us that two elements are always at work in salvation: our part and God's part.

Our part is to return. Until Judah gives up her lovers, she simply cannot return! Repentance is not so much a command as it is a description of what returning to the Lord looks like. Grace is free and salvation is a gift. But we must leave our lovers and come home to God to receive what He wants to give us.

God's part is to heal our wayward, deceitful, divided hearts. Until our hearts are cured (Jeremiah 17:9–10), we will continue to struggle with wandering thoughts, wayward desires, and lustful tendencies. But God can cure us of backsliding. He can heal our adulterous hearts.

Behold, the days are coming, declares the LORD, when I will make a new covenant with the house of Israel and the house of Judah, not like the covenant that I made with their fathers on the day when I took them by the hand to bring them out of the land of Egypt, my covenant that they broke, though I was their husband, declares the LORD. For this is the covenant that I will make with the house of Israel after those days, declares the LORD: I will put my law within them, and I will write it on their hearts. And I will be their God, and they shall be my people. And no longer shall each one teach his neighbor and each his brother, saying, 'Know the LORD,' for they shall all know me, from the least of them to the greatest, declares the LORD. For I will forgive their iniquity, and I will remember their sin no more. (Jeremiah 31:31–34)

Our part is to come home. God's part is to heal and transform our inner nature. When we confess the adulterous desires that lurk within, put away our lovers, and ask God to forgive our sin, then God is able to do a work of grace within us that purifies and unifies our hearts. Then we can love the Lord with our whole being!

A HYMN FOR BACKSLIDERS

During the eighteenth-century revival, John and Charles Wesley discovered backsliding was not just a doctrine to be debated, but a tragic reality that needed a pastoral response. In 1740, Charles Wesley wrote a hymn "for mourners convinced of backsliding," which was included in the early Methodist hymnals. Although the Wesley brothers preached passionately on the blessed assurance of sins forgiven, they recognized that falling from grace remained a real possibility throughout life.

DEPTH OF MERCY

Depth of mercy! Can there be
Mercy still reserved for me?
Can my God His wrath forbear,
Me, the chief of sinners, spare?

I have long withstood His grace,
Long provoked Him to His face,
Would not hearken to His calls,
Grieved Him by a thousand falls.

I have spilt His precious blood,
Trampled on the Son of God,
Filled with pangs unspeakable,
I, who yet am not in hell!

I my Master have denied,
I afresh have crucified,
And profaned His hallowed Name,
Put Him to an open shame....

If I rightly read Thy heart,
If Thou all compassion art,
Bow Thine ear, in mercy bow,
Pardon and accept me now.

Jesus speaks, and pleads His blood!
He disarms the wrath of God;
Now my Father's mercies move,
Justice lingers into love....

There for me my savior stands,
Holding forth His wounded hands;
God is love! I know, I feel,
Jesus weeps and loves me still....

Now incline me to repent,
Let me now my sins lament,
Now my foul revolt deplore,
Weep, believe, and sin no more.

http://cyberhymnal.org/htm/d/e/depthmer.htm

Questions for Discussion

1. Have you ever known someone personally who has experienced the consequences of adultery? Describe what that was like.

2. What happened to the 10 "lost tribes" of Israel? Did God really "divorce" them?

3. How do you understand the believer's security? Once saved, can a person fall from grace?

4. Discuss the difference between a "one-night stand" (momentary sin) and a long-term adulterous relationship (willful, continual sin). When does an adulterer reach the point of no return? Apply this understanding to salvation.

5. Does God have moral dilemmas (Should I divorce or should I reconcile? Should I condemn or should I save?)? How does your answer affect your concept of God?

6. Can God really heal the heart so that its lustful, adulterous tendencies are no longer present?

TOXIC CHURCH

Jeremiah 7:1—8:17

Where would you say is the riskiest place one could catch a life-threatening infection? An African jungle? A crowded New York subway? A kindergarten classroom? Think again. Scientific studies consistently tell us that the most dangerous place one can be to catch a deadly disease is the hospital!

According to the World Health Organization, "Hundreds of millions of patients are affected by health care-associated infections worldwide each year…and they account for 99,000 deaths in the USA."[2] Hospital-acquired infections are a reality that both patients and healthcare workers should take seriously. But awareness of this danger should not cause one to avoid hospitals. Rather, those who enter the doors should be aware that these buildings contain germs that have the potential to steal one's health and take one's life. Therefore, be alert and wash often.

Where would you say is the riskiest place one could acquire a soul-threatening spiritual infection? Las Vegas? Wall Street? Hollywood? Harvard? Think again. The place where one is most in danger of contracting a deadly spiritual virus is the church! Yes,

2. "Health care-associated infections: fact sheet", www.who.int/gpsc/country_work/gpsc_ccisc_fact_sheet_en.pdf (accessed 23 January 2017).

it's true. Becoming part of a religious community means you are exposing yourself to deadly spiritual germs. In fact, the spiritual diseases lurking inside the church sometimes are worse than those outside; however, such awareness should not keep you away from church. The body of Christ is designed for sinners like you and me. But those who spend time in religious communities need to be careful. Don't be naïve. These places are potentially toxic! So be alert and wash often.

JEREMIAH'S TEMPLE SERMON

If Jeremiah's sermon on spiritual adultery (2:1—4:4) caused him to be vilified, ostracized, and rejected, his Temple sermon (7:1—8:17) made him even more unpopular. As a priest (1:1), he should have had access to the Temple and his ministry should have been welcomed there. But God knew the message His prophet was going to give would be volatile and controversial, so He tells Jeremiah to "stand in the gate of the LORD's house" (7:2) and preach to the people as they arrive for worship. Jeremiah's job is to warn the worshipers as they go inside to be careful. It's toxic in there! In fact, the germs inside the Temple are more dangerous than those outside.

The word that came to Jeremiah from the LORD: "Stand in the gate of the LORD's house, and proclaim there this word, and say, Hear the word of the LORD, all you men of Judah who enter these gates to worship the Lord. Thus says the LORD of hosts, the God of Israel: Amend your ways and your deeds, and I will let you dwell in this place. Do not trust in these deceptive words: 'This is the temple of the LORD, the temple of the LORD, the temple of the LORD.' For if you truly amend

your ways and your deeds, if you truly execute justice one with another, if you do not oppress the sojourner, the fatherless, or the widow, or shed innocent blood in this place, and if you do not go after other gods to your own harm, then I will let you dwell in this place, in the land that I gave of old to your fathers forever. Behold, you trust in deceptive words to no avail."
(Jeremiah 7:1–8)

As a seminary student, I learned from my homiletics professor the importance of a sermon's introduction. The opening words of a message should be warm, engaging, and inviting. Personal stories, illustrations, and even the use of humor are helpful tools to use so listeners can feel comfortable and receptive. The introduction should let the audience know that what they are about to hear is going to help them lead happier and more productive lives.

Apparently, Jeremiah didn't have the same professor I did! Wasting no time, he gets right to the point: Amend your ways. Turn or burn. Jeremiah tells them wrath and judgment will fall on the Temple unless they repent and get right with God. He is telling the worshipers that the real problem facing the nation is *not* to be found in external threats: Babylon, pagan religions, corrupt governments, and so on. The real problem is not "out there" at all. The real problem is here in the Temple of the one true God! Jeremiah is shaking his prophetic finger at his congregation and shouting, "*You* are the problem!"

At the heart of Jeremiah's message is a warning *not* to trust the preachers inside. Their words are "deceptive" (7:4, 8). Their sermons are toxic. Although they are good speakers and their messages are full of comforting words, they are not to be trusted. They are guilty of pastoral malpractice!

One of the homiletical skills these false prophets had perfected in Jeremiah's day was the use of repetition. Whether preached from pulpits or sung in praise choruses, the audience was manipulated by repeating soothing words over and over.

- "This is the temple of the LORD, the temple of the LORD, the temple of the LORD" (7:4).
- "Peace, peace" (6:14; 8:11).
- "I have dreamed, I have dreamed" (23:25).

In Jeremiah's day, when the barbarians were at the gates and things were falling apart, people loved this kind of preaching. It reassured them that things were going to be okay. After hearing such messages, people went home feeling so much better. But Jeremiah recognizes the truth; these are false preachers preaching a false message. Pious platitudes and empty promises of better days ahead are not sufficient for times like these. So, he warns the people: Don't listen to these toxic preachers! Their sermons are full of deceptive words: "They have healed the wound of my people lightly, saying, 'Peace, peace,' when there is no peace" (8:11).

An appalling and horrible thing
has happened in the land:
the prophets prophesy falsely,
and the priests rule at their direction;
my people love to have it so,
but what will you do when the end comes? (Jeremiah 5:30–31)

In his sermon, Jeremiah exposes the hypocrisy in the lives of the worshipers. They claim to worship the God who is holy, holy, holy and yet their lives are sinful, sinful, sinful. Although Temple worship was supposed to be where people confessed their sins and found grace to turn from their evil ways, Jeremiah points out that for these worshipers, nothing could be further from the truth. These people come to church because they want to be comforted *in* their sins rather than finding deliverance *from* their sins.

Will you steal, murder, commit adultery, swear false-ly, make offerings to Baal, and go after other gods that you have not known, and then come and stand before me in this house, which is called by my name, and say, "We are delivered!"—only to go on doing all these abominations? Has this house, which is called by my name, become a den of robbers in your eyes? Behold, I myself have seen it, declares the LORD.
(Jeremiah 7:9–11)

It is obvious that worship has no impact on the daily lives and moral behavior of these people brazenly breaking at least half of the Ten Commandments. Jeremiah wants them to understand that it is simply impossible to worship a holy God and continue to live an unholy life! He is appalled at the toxicity of a religious environment that permits and promotes such irrational and contradictory behavior.

In one of his most provocative statements, Jeremiah compares these worshipers going to the Temple with robbers going to their dens (7:11). Jesus also found this analogy helpful in dealing with the toxic religious hypocrisy of his day (Mark 11:17). Many people go to church for the same reason robbers go to their caves: to hide! A den of robbers is a hideout, a place to conceal things. Although worship is intended to be a place where people come into the light and walk in the truth, for many it is just the opposite. This is where they hide, live in denial, and play games. Where better to pretend to be what one is not? Where better to hide from the truth? Where better to perpetuate a lie? Such people come to church, carry their Bibles, lift their hands in praise, and take notes on the sermon. Who would ever suspect that during the other six days of the week they are actually breaking over half of the Ten Commandments? In fact, these worshipers have mastered the art of deception so well that they convince not only others they are right with God but also themselves!

In his book *People of the Lie*, psychiatrist M. Scott Peck describes how evil does its worst when it masquerades as something good. This explains why evil people are sometimes very active in church. "It is not their sins per se that characterize evil people…the central defect of the evil is not the sin but the refusal to acknowledge it."[3] Peck goes on:

> *While they seem to lack any motivation to be good, they intensely desire to appear good. Their "goodness" is all on a level of pretense. It is, in effect, a lie. That is why they are the "people of the lie*[4] *(emphases mine).*

To illustrate the gravity of the situation, Jeremiah urges his listeners to take a field trip to Shiloh (7:12–15). Although the Tabernacle once had been located there, it is now a heap of ruins. Reciting repetitiously "this is the temple of the Lord" didn't save Shiloh from destruction! So, do they really think God will spare the Temple in Jerusalem? Do they imagine they are immune from wrath and judgment when they are even more corrupt than their ancestors at Shiloh?

---

3. M. Scott Peck, *People of the Lie* (New York: Simon & Schuster, 1983), 69.
4. Ibid., 75.

I will do to the house that is called by my name, and in which you trust, and to the place that I gave to you and to your fathers, as I did to Shiloh. And I will cast you out of my sight, as I cast out all your kinsmen, all the offspring of Ephraim. (Jeremiah 7:14–15)

Although the people of Jerusalem are guilty of many sins, Jeremiah focuses especially on two: idol worship and child sacrifice (7:30–31). These sins are especially an abomination in the sight of God. In fact, the thought of sacrificing children to idols is such a horrific notion that when God mentions the practice, He adds the words, "which I did not command, nor did it come into my mind" (7:31; see also 19:5; 32:35). When a nation offers its children to gods who cannot save (whether to Topheth, Baal, or Molech; or more contemporary idols such as sports, education, success, beauty, and so on), then you can be sure things are falling apart and the barbarians are at the gates.

Perhaps the most shocking reality of this whole sordid picture is the fact that Jerusalem is unaware of her sinful condition! The people are blind to the contradictory hypocrisy so evident in their lives. The worshipers piously claim, "We are wise, and the law of the LORD is with us" (Jeremiah 8:8). Their self-deception makes them unaware of the toxic condition of their worship.

The situation in Jerusalem is so bleak and the toxicity in the Temple is so great God tells Jeremiah not to even pray for these people for He will "not hear you" (7:16). The people who claim to know God have lived a lie for so long and their deception is so great that "truth has perished" (7:28).

Characteristics of a Toxic Church

Jeremiah's sermon can be summarized by highlighting five characteristics of a toxic church. While the Temple in Jerusalem is perhaps the most famous example of a poisonous spiritual environment, it is certainly not the only one.

Words Are Divorced from Truth

A toxic church is a place where "deceptive words" (Jeremiah 7:4, 8) are both preached by the clergy and believed by the people. The problem is not that the words are false but rather that they are misleading. A half-truth is more dangerous than a lie. "This is the temple of the LORD, the temple of the LORD, the temple of the LORD" and "Peace, peace" are truthful words in and of themselves. But these words become deceptive when placed in the mouths of hypocrites.

> *I never sent these prophets, but they ran anyway.*
> *I never spoke to them, but they preached away.*
> *If they'd have bothered to sit down and meet with me,*
> *they'd have preached my Message to my people.*
> *They'd have gotten them back on the right track,*
> *gotten them out of their evil ruts.* (Jeremiah 23:21–22 MSG)

When "deceptive words" are preached from the pulpit and believed in the pew, then the Day of Judgment is near. When pastors preach to make people happy rather than holy, then the barbarians are at the gates. When the clergy works to reassure people *in* their sins rather than announce deliverance *from* their sins, then the church is toxic indeed.

Worship Is Divorced from Obedience

In a toxic spiritual environment people may claim to have intense worship experiences and yet be living in willful, habitual patterns of sin (Jeremiah 7:8–10). Church becomes a place where people hide from the light of God's holiness rather than allowing it to expose the truth. Such an environment is toxic. It does more harm than good. God loathes such religious gatherings!

> I hate, I despise your feasts,
> and I take no delight in your solemn assemblies.
> Even though you offer me your burnt offerings and grain
> offerings, I will not accept them;
> and the peace offerings of your fattened animals,
> I will not look upon them.
> Take away from me the noise of your songs;
> to the melody of your harps I will not listen.
> But let justice roll down like waters,
> and righteousness like an ever-flowing stream. (Amos 5:21–24)

American churches in recent years have placed an emphasis on "contemporary" worship and the importance of being "seeker friendly." The result often has been an environment where worship is divorced from obedience. The church should quit entertaining the goats and get back to the job of feeding the sheep.

Life Is Divorced from Reality

When the pulpits of the land are filled with people pleasers rather than prophets of God, truth dies (Jeremiah 7:28). The culture no longer has a moral compass pointing true north. Without such a fixed point, people simply cannot find their moral bearings in a stormy sea. Consequently, everyone begins to do what is right in his own eyes (Judges 21:25). The result is cultural chaos, yet pastors continue to preach "Peace, peace!" In such a world, good is called evil and evil is called good (Isaiah 5:20). Bitter is mistaken for sweet, darkness is taken as light, and saints are vilified as sinners while sinners are lauded as saints. Life has become disconnected from reality. Welcome to *La-La Land*.

> *The church should quit entertaining the goats and get back to the job of feeding the sheep.*

There Is Clergy Malpractice

There were many popular preachers in Jeremiah's day: Pashhur (Jeremiah 20:1–6), Hananiah (Jeremiah 28:1–17), Ahab, Zedekiah, and Shemaiah (Jeremiah 29:21–32). Tragically, they were all false prophets, preaching deceptive words. Calling them by name, Jeremiah warns the people not to listen to them or believe what they say, not to fall for their pious platitudes and soothing messages of peace. Jeremiah emphasizes two criteria helpful in discerning true prophets from false ones: their character and the content of their message.

Their character. "Both prophet and priest are ungodly; even in my house I have found their evil, declares the LORD" (Jeremiah 23:11). In Jeremiah's day—as in our own—two sins are prominent: greed for money (Jeremiah 8:10) and sexual immorality (Jeremiah 23:14; 29:21–23). Jeremiah knows hypocrisy in the pulpit leads to moral chaos in the nation.

Their message. The false prophets Jeremiah warns about are essentially good preachers. Their oratorical skills are impressive and much of what they say sounds orthodox and brings comfort to their listeners. But if you examine the content of their message, you begin to discover the error of their teaching:

1. They claim to be God's messengers, yet God had neither called them nor taught them what to say (Jeremiah 23:21–22). Their sermons are simply the product of their own imaginations. They make them up as they go along. Their message is from man, not from God.

> *Don't listen to the sermons of the prophets.*
> *It's all hot air. Lies, lies, and more lies. They make it all up.*
> *Not a word they speak comes from me.*
> *They preach their "Everything Will Turn Out Fine" sermon*
> *to congregations with no taste for God,*
> *Their "Nothing Bad Will Ever Happen to You" sermon*
> *to people who are set in their own ways.*
> (Jeremiah 23:16–17 MSG)

2. They offer the people false assurance and security, claiming all is well when judgment is about to fall on the land. Although their words bring a measure of comfort ("Peace, peace"), it is a deceptive message. A doctor who prescribes poison is not as dangerous as a preacher who preaches error.

> *I said, "But Master, GOD! Their preachers have been telling them that everything is going to be all right—no war and no famine—that there's nothing to worry about."*

> *Then GOD said, "These preachers are liars, and they use my name to cover their lies. I never sent them, I never commanded them, and I don't talk with them. The sermons they've been handing out are sheer illusion, tissues of lies, whistlings in the dark."*
> (Jeremiah 14:13–14 MSG)

3. Their words are soothing, sentimental, and sugarcoated. Like cotton candy, their words taste sweet but have no substance. Rather than proclaiming the truth, these preachers offer religious clichés and pious platitudes.

> *"You prophets who do nothing but dream—*
> *go ahead and tell your silly dreams.*
> *But you prophets who have a message from me—*
> *tell it truly and faithfully.*
> *What does straw have in common with wheat?*
> *Nothing else is like GOD's Decree.*
> *Isn't my Message like fire?" GOD's Decree.*
> *"Isn't it like a sledgehammer busting a rock?"*
> (Jeremiah 23:28–29 MSG)

4. They are guilty of plagiarism. Rather than basing their messages in the revealed Word of God, they copy their sermons from one another.

> *"I've had it with the 'prophets' who get all their sermons secondhand from each other. Yes, I've had it with them. They make up stuff and then pretend it's a real sermon."* (Jeremiah 23:30–31 MSG)

These false prophets of the true God are more dangerous than the true prophets of false gods! Just as contaminated medicine is more dangerous than poison because people are more likely to swallow it, so a half-truth is more dangerous than a lie.

> *"Over in Samaria I saw prophets*
> *acting like silly fools—shocking!*
> *They preached using that no-god Baal for a text,*
> *messing with the minds of my people.*

And the Jerusalem prophets are even worse—horrible!—
  sex-driven, living a lie,
Subsidizing a culture of wickedness,
  and never giving it a second thought.
They're as bad as those wretches in old Sodom,
  the degenerates of old Gomorrah." (Jeremiah 23:13–14 MSG)

THE CHURCH DOES NOT KNOW IT IS TOXIC

Perhaps the most significant characteristic of a toxic church is this: a toxic church *does not know* it is a toxic church! The most dangerous hospital is not the one with germs lurking in the building, but rather the one that *does not know* it has germs lurking in the building! Ignorance can be fatal. The reason sins inside the church are so deadly is not because they are somehow worse than those outside. Rather, the reason is simply this: these sins are denied. "The heart is deceitful above all things, and desperately sick; who can understand it?" (Jeremiah 17:9)

Jeremiah's Temple sermon goes over like the proverbial lead balloon. Those who hear it rise up to reject both the message and the messenger. But over time, God's people realize the prophet is right! His words are true. His message is meant not to condemn them but to shake them awake and save them from the coming wrath.

Questions for Discussion

1. Have you ever been part of a toxic church environment? Have you ever been on the receiving end of clergy malpractice? Describe your experience.

2. Have you ever known a church that was like a den of robbers, a place to hide? Discuss that situation.

3. Which one of the five characteristics of a toxic church most closely resembles your present church community? What should you do about it?

4. Should a pastor understand his job to be one of comforting the afflicted or one of afflicting the comfortable? When is "Peace, peace" a bad sermon?

5. Does America practice child sacrifice? Do evangelical Christians?

6. Discuss your response to the statement that "the church should quit entertaining the goats and get back to the job of feeding the sheep."

WHY, OH WHY?

Jeremiah 12:1–5

Everyone, at some point in life, confronts the "Why?" question. Whether the question is provoked by birth defects, random violence, natural catastrophes, disease, famine, or some other human tragedy, all of us, at one time or another, look up to heaven and shout, "Why?" Deep inside, we seem to know intuitively that life is not supposed to be like this. The animal world doesn't seem particularly troubled by the fact of suffering and pain, but not so humans. When tragedy comes, we struggle to explain the inexplicable and develop philosophies and theologies that seek to answer life's most mysterious question.

Imagine how counselors from different religions and worldviews might attempt to comfort someone trying to deal with a tragic situation such as a diagnosis of cancer. A *Hindu* might say, "Bad things happen because of bad karma. Perhaps in a previous life you did something evil that merits this tragic consequence." A *Buddhist* would perhaps point out that the cause of suffering is our desire not to suffer. Therefore, if we would just snuff out all our desires our suffering would cease. A *Muslim* would insist that everything that happens is the will of Allah. Therefore, stop asking questions and just submit to his will for your life. An *evolutionist* would perhaps explain that this is simply how the law of the jungle works: the strong survive and the weak don't. An *atheist* might try to encourage you by saying, "There is no ultimate meaning in life; get over it and move on." It is obvious that answering the "Why?" question is not easy for any of us. Explaining why bad things happen and offering comfort to those who hurt is perhaps life's greatest challenge.

But for *Christians*, this question is especially problematic. This is true because the Christian faith is firmly rooted in two unshakeable beliefs about God: (1) He is absolute in goodness, and (2) He is absolute in power. Therefore, if something tragic happens, a Christian is thrown on the horns of a dilemma: either God *could* do something if only He *would* (He is powerful but not good) or God *would* do something if only He *could* (He is good but not powerful). So, when a Christian is confronted with suffering, he or she must deal not only with the tragedy itself but also with the existential pain that comes in asking the question, "Where are You, God? Are You good? Are You powerful? If You are, then why did this tragedy happen?" Seeking an answer to this question can be as traumatic as dealing with the crisis itself. In fact, this question lies at the root of why many choose to reject God altogether and live in unbelief. This explains why some call the problem of suffering "the rock of atheism."

DISAPPOINTMENT WITH GOD

The twelfth chapter of Jeremiah describes a season of the prophet's life when he simply cannot take any more. Life isn't working out like he thinks it should and he knows God is responsible! The barbarians are at the gates, the government is corrupt, the citizens of Judah are playing *Trivial Pursuit*, and the church is asleep. Although Jeremiah is obeying the call on his life to be a prophet in such a situation, his message is being rejected and he is being persecuted. Worse yet, the false prophets are popular with the people and living in comfort and material prosperity.

Jeremiah simply has no categories to account for why an all-loving and all-powerful God would allow such a tragic situation to develop. But what can he do? Atheism is no option, nor is turning to other gods or religions. Jeremiah chooses the only path he feels is left open: he decides to take God to court and sue Him for malpractice! He puts God in the witness stand and demands that He give an account for His actions. C. S. Lewis describes a similar situation:

> *The ancient man approached God as the accused person approaches his judge. For the modern man the roles are reversed. He is the judge: God is in the dock. He is quite a kindly judge: if God should have a reasonable defense for being the god who permits war, poverty and disease, he is ready to listen to it. The trial may even end in God's acquittal. But the important thing is that Man is on the Bench and God in the Dock.[5]*

In this chapter, Jeremiah is taking a similar posture with God. The context is a courtroom; the language is litigious. Although Jeremiah knows God is really the judge, he treats Him like the accused. Acting in the role of prosecuting attorney, Jeremiah points his finger at God and says:

> *You are always righteous, LORD, when I bring a case before you.*
> *Yet I would speak with you about your justice:*
> *Why does the way of the wicked prosper?*
> *Why do all the faithless live at ease?*

5. C. S. Lewis. *God in the Dock: Essays on Theology and Ethics* (Grand Rapids: Eerdmans, 1970), 244.

*You have planted them, and they have taken root; they grow
and bear fruit.*

You are always on their lips but far from their hearts.

(Jeremiah 12:1–2 NIV)

Jeremiah is speaking to the judge of all the earth about His justice! The wicked are prospering and the righteous are suffering. Is this any way to run the universe? Hadn't God promised to uproot the wicked (Jeremiah 1:10)? Yet now it appears He has planted them and they have taken root. They are growing and bearing fruit! "Lord, these things ought not to be! Why, oh why?"

COMPETING WITH HORSES

Perhaps the prophet felt some emotional release just daring to ask his question to God. After all, when questions are unexpressed they sometimes fester and provoke cynicism and doubt. There is something therapeutic about telling God what we really feel, even when it sounds accusatory.

But when you dare to be honest and candid with God, watch out. God may respond by being honest and candid with you! God answers Jeremiah's questions with a few questions of His own. He does not remain in the defendant's chair. Retaking His rightful place as judge, God looks down at Jeremiah, puts His sovereign finger in the prophet's chest, and says, "All right, little man; you've asked your questions, now you listen while I ask Mine!"

> *"If you have raced with men on foot and they have worn you out,
> how can you compete with horses?*
> *If you stumble in safe country,
> how will you manage in the thickets by the Jordan?"*
> (Jeremiah 12:5 NIV)

Say what? Jeremiah had asked, "Why do the wicked prosper?" God answers, "Can you compete with horses?" What kind of an answer is that? Jeremiah must have wondered if God heard his question at all!

By asking Jeremiah how he would fare in a race with horses, God is reminding His prophet of the fact that sometimes life isn't fair, so get over it! Jeremiah is a man-sized prophet wrestling with God-sized questions. He may be able to hold his own in a footrace with other men, but what will he do when he finds himself racing in the Kentucky Derby? In other words, he may think things are bad now, but wait until the Babylonian army arrives. You ain't seen nothin' yet!

This is close to the answer God gives Job. After suffering the loss of his possessions, his children, and his health, Job wants to know "Why?" Although Job finds himself in conflict with his comforters over how to explain the tragedy of his life, his real problem is not with his comforters and their questionable theology. His real problem is with God! "Lord, I've trusted You and sought to follow You all my life and yet I've suffered the loss of everything. Why, oh why? I want an answer! Please explain to me why all this happened!"

After listening to Job and his comforters debate the problem of suffering for 37 chapters, God finally speaks. Basically, He says, "Okay, you've had your chance to ask *your* questions. Now you sit still and listen while I ask *Mine!*"

Then the LORD answered Job out of the whirlwind and said:
"Who is this that darkens counsel by words without knowledge?
Dress for action like a man;
I will question you, and you make it known to me.

*"Where were you when I laid the foundation of the earth?
Tell me, if you have understanding.
Who determined its measurements—surely you know!*
(Job 38:1–5)

*Can you lift up your voice to the clouds,
that a flood of waters may cover you?
Can you send forth lightnings, that they may go
and say to you, 'Here we are'?* (Job 38:34–35)

*Is it by your understanding that the hawk soars
and spreads his wings toward the south?
Is it at your command that the eagle mounts up
and makes his nest on high?* (Job 39:26–27)

*Dress for action like a man;
I will question you, and you make it known to me.
Will you even put me in the wrong?
Will you condemn me that you may be in the right?
Have you an arm like God,
and can you thunder with a voice like his?* (Job 40:7–9)

*Can you draw out Leviathan with a fishhook
or press down his tongue with a cord?
Can you put a rope in his nose
or pierce his jaw with a hook?...
Will you play with him as with a bird,
or will you put him on a leash for your girls?"* (Job 41:1–2, 5)

Then Job answered the Lord *and said:
"I know that you can do all things,
and that no purpose of yours can be thwarted....
Therefore I have uttered what I did not understand,*

things too wonderful for me, which I did not know....
I had heard of you by the hearing of the ear,
but now my eye sees you;
therefore I despise myself, and repent in dust and ashes."
(Job 42:1–6)

God sometimes answers our questions by asking us questions! While this may not be the kind of answer we are looking for, it does help to put us in our place and remind us that God is God. He doesn't always choose to explain why He does what He does. "For as the heavens are higher than the earth, so are my ways higher than your ways and my thoughts than your thoughts" (Isaiah 55:9).

THREE CLUES TO THE MEANING OF SUFFERING

The twelfth chapter of Jeremiah is a marvelous passage for anyone who has ever been disappointed with God or felt He wasn't performing the way He ought. It helps us to make sense of what doesn't make sense. The Bible may not answer all our intellectual questions, but it does point us in the right direction to find real help. This passage reminds us that suffering is not so much a problem to be solved as it is a mystery to be embraced! God responds to Jeremiah's questions about why bad things happen by offering four clues to the meaning of suffering.

Our Real Struggle in Life Is with God

As things were falling apart in Jeremiah's world, he struggled on many different fronts: with the false prophets, with corrupt government leaders, with a nation that would not listen to the truth, with the Babylonians, and so on. But deep in his heart of hearts he knew his real conflict was not with any of these. His real struggle was with God! "God, if You are truly sovereign and if You are truly good, then why are these awful things happening? Why, oh why?" Jeremiah has a solid enough relationship with God to look Him in the face and say, *"I would speak with you about your justice"* (Jeremiah 12:1 NIV).

Although many in the church today would be horrified to hear someone praying to God with such candor, the Bible is full of examples of heroes of the faith who speak plainly to God, pleading with Him to explain why things are falling apart all around them!

- *Jacob,* in a wrestling match with God, prays: *"I will not let you go unless you bless me"* (Genesis 32:26).

- After a season of great frustration while leading a people who only complained, *Moses* prays: *"I am not able to carry all this people alone; the burden is too heavy for me. If you will treat me like this, kill me at once"* (Numbers 11:14–15).

- In the middle of his suffering, *Job* cries out, *"I loathe my life; I will give free utterance to my complaint; I will speak in the bitterness of my soul. I will say to God, Do not condemn me; let me know why you contend against me. Does it seem good to you to oppress, to despise the work of your hands and favor the designs of the wicked?...Your hands fashioned and made me, and now you have destroyed me altogether...leave me alone, that I may find a little cheer"* (Job 10:1–3, 8, 20).

- The *psalmist* prays, *"O LORD, why do you cast my soul away? Why do you hide your face from me?"* (Psalm 88:14)

Yes, the Bible gives us permission to speak candidly with God and ask Him our deepest questions. We can share our deepest doubts and fears with the One who loves us. Since He alone is God and sovereign over all, we are free to hold Him responsible for everything happening in our lives, even the tragedies and losses that torment us. "Lord, why, oh why?" The first clue to the mystery of suffering is the need to be honest and face the truth that our real difficulty is not with the circumstances of our pain but with the One who is allowing it to happen!

We Can Tell God How We Really Feel

For contemporary Christians, the language Jeremiah uses to talk to God is startling, even scandalous. Not only in chapter 12, but throughout the book, Jeremiah has the audacity to tell God what he is really thinking and feeling. When Jerusalem is attacked and destroyed, Jeremiah says, "Ah, Lord GOD, surely you have utterly deceived this people and Jerusalem, saying, 'It shall be well with you,' whereas the sword has reached their very life" (Jeremiah 4:10). When he obeys God, doing what is right and then everything falls apart, he asks God, "Will you be to me like a deceitful brook, like waters that fail?" (Jeremiah 15:18). On another occasion he is even more blunt: "O LORD, you have deceived me, and I was deceived" (Jeremiah 20:7). When his enemies gang up against him, Jeremiah vents his frustration by telling God to "deliver up their children to famine... let their wives become childless and widowed. May their men meet death by pestilence, their youths be struck down by the sword in battle" (Jeremiah 18:21). When he is in a deep pit of depression and despair, he cries out to God, *"Cursed be the day on which I was born!... Why did I come out from the womb to see toil and sorrow, and spend my days in shame?"* (Jeremiah 20:14, 18)

Although we may be disturbed by how shockingly honest Jeremiah is with God, we must recognize that the Bible is full of similar examples of saints who had a close enough relationship with God that they felt free to pour out their innermost thoughts to the One who loved them. People in healthy marriages learn that speaking one's heart candidly to one's spouse does not mean the marriage is about to break. No!

It indicates that the relationship is strong enough to bear the weight of naked emotional honesty in its rawest expression. Listen to other examples from Scripture of such honest conversations with God:

- The psalmist (Asaph) complains to God that the wicked in his day are prospering and blurts, *"All in vain have I kept my heart clean."* (Psalm 73:13)

- After waiting and waiting for God to act, the prophet Habakkuk asks, *"O LORD, how long shall I cry for help, and you will not hear? Or cry to you 'Violence!' and you will not save? Why do you make me see iniquity, and why do you idly look at wrong?"* (Habakkuk 1:2–3)

- Sitting in prison awaiting execution, John the Baptist sends a messenger to Jesus, asking, *"Are you the one who is to come, or shall we look for another?"* (Matthew 11:3)

- Even the sinless Jesus, on the cross, screams out in his suffering, *"My God, my God, why have you forsaken me?"* (Mark 15:34)

Many evangelical Christians today are emotionally dishonest. Acknowledging what they are *really* feeling and thinking is simply too shocking for them, so they find ways to deny the truth and live a life of make-believe. Those who do find the courage to confront what they are really feeling often choose to first pour out their hearts to a therapist. But why not follow Jeremiah's example and begin by telling God Himself what is really going on inside? He already knows! Although we are warned not to "grumble" as the Hebrews did during their wanderings in the wilderness, we are encouraged to come humbly and honestly into His presence and the safety of His love, and pour out our hearts before Him.

When We Get Honest with God, God Will Get Honest with Us

When we tell God what is really on our hearts, He will tell us what is really on His heart. Jeremiah blurts out to God, "Why does the way of the wicked prosper?" (Jeremiah 12:1). I can imagine such candor with God had a cathartic effect and caused Jeremiah to feel better. But watch out! Candid conversation is a two-way street. When we are honest and confess what is in our hearts, God returns the favor! "Okay, you've asked Me the question burning in *your* heart. Now let Me be candid and ask you the question burning in Mine!"

If you have raced with men on foot, and they have wearied you, how will you compete with horses? And if in a safe land you are so trusting, what will you do in the thicket of the Jordan? (Jeremiah 12:5)

God takes personal relationships seriously. He has emotions too! The third clue to the meaning of suffering is that when we get candid and honest with God, then God gets candid and honest with us.

TRUST IN THE LORD ANYWAY

Jeremiah learns an important lesson when he pours out his questions before God. It is okay to express your doubts and fears to God, but it is not okay to stay in doubt and fear! Transparent honesty before God is meant to get the poison of bitterness and doubt out of us. The whole point of candid conversation with God is to arrive at a place of deep trust and confidence. God is in control. He knows what He is doing, and it is good, even if it doesn't make sense. So, wait on the Lord and trust in His promises. Later in this same chapter, God underscores once again His promise to Jeremiah and to Jerusalem. The wicked ultimately will not prosper, and one day the righteous will reign in glory.

Thus says the LORD *concerning all my evil neighbors who touch the heritage that I have given my people Israel to inherit: "Behold, I will pluck them up from their land, and I will pluck up the house of Judah from among them. And after I have plucked them up, I will again have compassion on them, and I will bring them again each to his heritage and each to his land. And it shall come to pass, if they will diligently learn the ways of my people, to swear by my name, 'As the* LORD *lives,' even as they taught my people to swear by Baal, then they shall be built up in the midst of my people. But if any nation will not listen, then I will utterly pluck it up and destroy it, declares the* LORD*."* (Jeremiah 12:14–17)

The moral of the story is this: trust in the Lord and His promises, even when things are falling apart all around you! Faith means believing in advance what will only make sense in reverse. In 1774, the English poet William Cowper wrote a hymn that expresses beautifully the mystery of suffering. It is titled "God Moves in a Mysterious Way."

GOD MOVES IN A MYSTERIOUS WAY

God moves in a mysterious way
His wonders to perform;
He plants His footsteps in the sea
And rides upon the storm.

Deep in unfathomable mines
Of never failing skill,
He treasures up His bright designs
And works His sovereign will.

Ye fearful saints, fresh courage take;
The clouds ye so much dread
Are big with mercy and shall break
In blessings on your head.

Judge not the Lord by feeble sense,
But trust Him for His grace;
Behind a frowning providence
He hides a smiling face.

His purposes will ripen fast,
Unfolding every hour;
The bud may have a bitter taste,
But sweet will be the flower.

Blind unbelief is sure to err
And scan His work in vain;
God is His own interpreter,
And He will make it plain.

http://www.cyberhymnal.org/htm/g/m/gmovesmw.htm

Questions for Discussion

1. What did you learn from this lesson that you did not know before?

2. Think about the prayer meetings you attend. Do people have freedom to talk candidly to God and express what they are really feeling? Do you? Why or why not?

3. Have you ever been disappointed with God, feeling He hadn't performed like you thought He should? How did you respond? Did the experience make your faith stronger or weaker?

4. Some people approach suffering as if it were a problem to be solved. Others approach suffering as if it were a mystery to be embraced. Who is right?

5. How does the cross of Jesus help us deal with suffering?

6. What was Cowper trying to say with his hymn? Which stanza speaks to you the most?

The Potter's House

Jeremiah 18—19

Perhaps you heard the story of the Calvinist who dreamed he died and went to heaven. He found himself standing before two doors. One door said, "Enter Here All Who Are Elect and Predestined to Salvation." The other door said, "Enter Here All Who Freely Choose Salvation." The Calvinist chose the first door. An angel standing at the door asked him why he had come. "I *chose* to come here," replied the Calvinist. Frowning, the angel pointed to the other door. Arriving at this door, another angel asked why he had come. The man answered, "I had no choice." With a scowl, the angel pointed back to the other door. In his dream, now become a nightmare, the Calvinist envisioned himself shuffling back and forth between the two doors for all eternity.

The story is silly but illustrates well one of the greatest debates in theology: how to reconcile God's sovereignty and human freedom. If God, in His sovereign power has decreed everything that is and that will be, then how is it possible that humans are free? But if humans are truly free, then how is it possible that God is in control? You can be sure that Calvinists are not the only ones having nightmares. Wesleyans, too, toss on their beds trying to resolve one of the deepest mysteries of life.

When one examines the Scriptures, two inescapable truths leap from the sacred page. On the one hand, God is absolutely sovereign in His purposes and plans. His will is immutable (unchanging) and nothing can thwart the accomplishment of His designs. As the psalmist says, "Our God is in heaven; he does whatever pleases him" (Psalm 115:3 NIV). On the other hand, men and women are held fully responsible for their choices. They choose to believe or not believe, to obey or disobey, to say yes or no. And their choices have moral significance. Over and over again in the Bible, men are encouraged to turn from their sins and put their trust in God. The assumption behind such exhortations is that humans have the capacity to choose and will be held accountable for their choices.

On the surface, these two truths seem to be contradictory and mutually exclusive. One must choose one or the other. Either we live in a world where everything is controlled by a sovereign God and everything is predetermined, or we live in a world where everything is up for grabs and man is the measure of all things. It is one or the other, right? Seeking to reconcile these two truths at both an intellectual and an experiential level is one of the most difficult challenges in life!

No passage of Scripture addresses this great mystery better than Jeremiah 18—19. Jeremiah's sermon on the Potter and the clay is the most famous sermon he ever preached. Like the parables of Jesus, it is as much visual as it is verbal. It is simple enough for a child to understand and profound enough for theologians to spend centuries plumbing its depths. It is perhaps the most astute analysis of the problem of human freedom and divine sovereignty ever written. Jeremiah's sermon is profoundly simple and simply profound!

It is unlikely that Jeremiah preached these two chapters on a single occasion. Apparently, this message of the Potter and the clay was a theme to which the prophet returned again and again. The compiler of the book organized this material into a single unit so that the message could come through in all its original power. The theme of the sermon is the simple fact that God is the Potter and Israel is the clay. So why can't He fashion the vessel He wants to make? Why can't He make a piece of pottery with which He is well pleased? Answering this question takes us to the very heart of the paradoxical tension that exists between divine sovereignty and human freedom.

The passage can be divided into two parts: what happens when the clay is wet (chapter 18), and what happens when the clay is dry (chapter 19).

PART ONE: WET CLAY

Jeremiah 18 contains the first part of the sermon: what God can do with wet clay. The primary message is nonverbal. The sermon is a visual object lesson.

> *The word that came to Jeremiah from the LORD: "Arise, and go down to the potter's house, and there I will let you hear my words." So I went down to the potter's house, and there he was working at his wheel. And the vessel he was making of clay was spoiled in the potter's hand, and he reworked it into another vessel, as it seemed good to the potter to do. Then the word of the LORD came to me, "O house of Israel, can I not do with you as this potter has done? declares the LORD. Behold, like the clay in the potter's hand, so are you in my hand, O house of Israel."* (Jeremiah 18:1–6)

At God's command, the prophet stands and quietly watches as the potter works at his wheel—spinning, shaping, adding water, and shaping some more. Nothing was more common in the Ancient Near East than a potter working with clay. What message could God possibly have for Israel from such a mundane occurrence? But Jeremiah keeps watching. Something isn't quite to the potter's liking. The clay is "spoiled." Perhaps a pebble is mixed in the clay. Maybe a bubble has formed, or perhaps the shape isn't quite what he wants. Rather than throwing the clay away in a fit of anger, the potter scoops up the lump of clay, adds more water, and starts again. He reworks it into a new shape, as it seems good to the potter to do.

Suddenly Jeremiah has a divine flash of insight! God's message is crystal clear. The prophet is never the same after this, and the impact of what he learns changes his ministry forever: The Potter (God) is sovereign over the clay (His people). He chooses the clay and decides in advance what He wants to make. With artistic majesty, He begins to shape the lump of dirt into a vessel that would bring Him joy. He has a predetermined plan for that lump of clay. He knows what it is *to be* and He knows what it is *to do*. But wait. Something isn't right. The clay is not turning out like He had hoped. Not a problem. The Potter adds more water and starts again.

Jeremiah's flash of insight came when God asked the question, "O house of Israel, can I not do with you as this potter has done?" Notice that God's words are in the form of a question. But answering the question, as Israel is about to find out, is harder than you think!

The next part of Jeremiah's sermon takes us even deeper into the mystery of how that divine sovereignty interacts with human freedom. God is speaking:

If at any time I declare concerning a nation or a kingdom, that I will pluck up and break down and destroy it, and if that nation, concerning which I have spoken, turns from its evil, I will relent of the disaster that I intended to do to it. And if at any time I declare concerning a nation or a kingdom that I will build and plant it, and if it does evil in my sight, not listening to my voice, then I will relent of the good that I had intended to do to it. Now, therefore, say to the men of Judah and the inhabitants of Jerusalem: 'Thus says the LORD, Behold, I am shaping disaster against you and devising a plan against you. Return, every one from his evil way, and amend your ways and your deeds.' (Jeremiah 18:7–11)

There is one crucial difference between a lump of clay on a potter's wheel and the lump of clay called man (Genesis 2:7): the man has a mind of his own! The Potter chooses us and has a predetermined plan, but unless we consent to remain on the wheel and allow Him to do His work in our lives, we will never take the shape He intends. Verses 7–12 reflect this sobering reality on an international scale. Using the if, then form of conditional argument, God pleads with the peoples of the earth to act responsibly in the face of divine sovereignty. If God says He is going to destroy you, then turn from your sins so that He won't. And if God says He is going to bless you, then for heaven's sake don't turn away from Him and do evil lest He change His plans and send judgment upon you. Yes, God is absolutely sovereign in His plans and in His ways. He is in total control. And yet you are completely responsible for your choices and will be held fully accountable.

Jeremiah's sermon provokes a strong negative reaction. *"It's no use. We will continue with our own plans; we will all follow the stubbornness of our evil hearts.... Come, let's make plans against Jeremiah...let's attack him with our tongues and pay no attention to anything he says"* (Jeremiah 18:12, 18 NIV). To preach divine sovereignty and human responsibility is not the way to become a popular preacher. Such a message typically provokes either a revival or a riot!

God has a strong response to their strong response: *"Ask among the nations, Who has heard the like of this?... Like the east wind I will scatter them before the enemy. I will show them my back, not my face, in the day of their calamity"* (Jeremiah 18:13, 17). God's sovereign majesty is maintained as He responds to the rebellious attitude of the willful clay.

PART TWO: DRY CLAY

The second part of Jeremiah's sermon also deals with pottery, but this time the clay is no longer wet on the wheel. It has hardened into a permanent shape.

> *Thus says the LORD, "Go, buy a potter's earthenware flask, and take some of the elders of the people and some of the elders of the priests, and go out to the Valley of the Son of Hinnom at the entry of the Potsherd Gate, and proclaim there the words that I tell you."* (Jeremiah 19:1–2)

The Potsherd Gate was where broken pottery was thrown out, a sort of town dump. The Valley of Hinnom[6] was the place where child sacrifice was practiced (Jeremiah 7:31; 32:35). Thus, we see that the backdrop for Jeremiah's sermon is full of symbolic significance. The sermon is found in verses 3–9 and is a prophetic

---

6. The Hebrew term *ge* (valley) *hinnom* is the origin of the Greek term *gehenna*, which is typically translated hell in the New Testament.

announcement of coming judgment on Jerusalem. Focusing specifically on the sins of forsaking God, worshiping idols, killing the innocent, and the horrible practice of child sacrifice (Jeremiah 19:4–5), Jeremiah announces that divine judgment is soon to fall on the wicked city of Jerusalem.

If the people had listened to the first part of Jeremiah's sermon (Jeremiah 18:7–11), they would have known judgment could be averted if only they would turn from their sins and repent. But alas, the people are so hardened in their sin that they would not (could not?) even pause to consider the consequences of their choices. They have taken a shape (like an earthenware flask) displeasing to their Maker. The final part of Jeremiah's sermon is a dramatic and symbolic action, illustrating the consequences of the people's choices.

> *"Then you shall break the flask in the sight of the men who go with you, and shall say to them, 'Thus says the LORD of hosts: So will I break this people and this city, as one breaks a potter's vessel, so that it can never be mended'. ...I am bringing upon this city and upon all its towns all the disaster that I have pronounced against it, because they have stiffened their neck, refusing to hear my words."* (Jeremiah 19:10–11, 15)

When clay hardens into a shape the potter never intended it to have, there is nothing to be done except to destroy it. Once hardened, adding water and getting it back on the wheel would be useless—the shape is permanent. The point of no return has been reached and the only thing left to do is break the vessel and toss the broken shards on the city dump.

Summarizing the Sermon

Let's summarize the message of Jeremiah's sermon by highlighting three sobering truths the prophet learns at the potter's house:

First, the potter has a *plan*. Even before he sits down at his wheel, the potter has a mental image of what he wants to create. It is amazing what a potter can do with dirt and water! God made Adam from dirt (Genesis 2:7), shaping him into a masterpiece reflecting the image of his Creator. Ever since that moment in the Garden of Eden, potters have used dirt to make amazing vessels of beauty and artistic design. The potter is not just a technician, making vessels that serve a pragmatic function. He is also an artist, making vessels of beauty, giving them shape and color. Archaeologists have discovered that even in the most ancient fragments of pottery unearthed, the shards reveal not just functional practicality but beauty and art. Jeremiah knew he had been "formed" by God for a divine purpose (Jeremiah 1:5). Therefore, it was easy for him to understand that God had a divine plan for other vessels too.

> *For we are his workmanship [Greek, poiema], created in Christ Jesus for good works, which God prepared beforehand, that we should walk in them.* (Ephesians 2:10)

Tragically, most people seem to wander through life never discovering the real purpose for which they were made. They get up, get dressed, go to work, come home, mow the grass, pay the bills, and go to bed. Then the next day they repeat the same motions. Many live like Sisyphus in Greek mythology, who was condemned to Hades, where his punishment was to roll a massive stone to the top of a hill. But once at the top, the stone would roll back to the bottom. Then poor Sisyphus would have to go through the motions again…and again…and again.

Before you were born, God envisioned a purpose for your life. Even before He sat down at the Potter's wheel, He knew what He wanted you to be and to do. Because He is sovereign, He is ready and able to do whatever it takes to ensure His purposes for your life are fulfilled. But for that to happen, you must remain on the Potter's wheel, allowing Him to work you and shape you as He sees fit. Sometimes this process will be painful as He presses and squeezes the clay. Sometimes He may decide to start all over again. But as you trust the Master's touch, spinning and turning, cooperating with the process, you can be assured He is accomplishing His sovereign purposes in you and ultimately through you.

The second truth Jeremiah learns is that the potter has a *problem*. As Jeremiah stands watching at the potter's house, he sees that the potter is not happy. Something is wrong. The vessel is "spoiled" (Jeremiah 18:4). The text does not tell us the exact nature of the problem, but the vessel is not turning out as the potter had hoped. For some reason, the clay is resistant to what the potter is doing.

> *But who are you, O man, to talk back to God? Shall what is formed say to him who formed it, "Why did you make me like this?" Does not the potter have the right to make out of the same lump of clay some pottery for noble purposes and some for common use?* (Romans 9:20–21 NIV1984)

Fortunately, the potter does not take the clay and angrily throw it out. No. He simply adds more water and starts the process again. Can't God do that with you? Won't you let Him simply do what He has always wanted to do in your life: fashion and shape you into a thing of beauty?

The frightening reality is this: If we refuse to cooperate with the Potter and begin to take a shape He never intended, we may reach a point of no return—when we harden into a shape even God Himself will not redeem. The consequences of such a reality are terrifying. Such a vessel has no use but to be shattered and the broken pieces scattered on the garbage dump of hell.

The third truth Jeremiah learns is that the potter has a *question*. It is significant that the divine Potter does not make a statement saying, "O house of Israel, I am going to do with you as this potter has done." No. He asks a question: "Can I not do with you as this potter has done?" (Jeremiah 18:6). The question demands an answer. God *wants* Israel to respond. Can't the sovereign Lord of the universe do what He wants? God also is waiting to hear what *you* will say. Your answer will reveal more about your true theology than any doctrinal creed you could recite. But far more important, your answer will seal your eternal destiny.

Yes, God is sovereign. He does whatever He wants. But all the power in the universe cannot forcibly bring about the one thing this Potter wants more than anything else: your love, your trust, and the surrender of your will to Him. If you will just get back on the wheel, He can fashion you into a thing of beauty. If you are resistant, get back on the wheel anyway! He can soften your heart and, through His grace working in you, He can enable you to love Him, to believe His promises, and to surrender your will. Yes, He is fully sovereign. And yes, you are fully responsible.

HAVE THINE OWN WAY, LORD

Have Thine own way, Lord!
Have Thine own way!
Thou art the Potter, I am the clay.
Mold me and make me after Thy will,
While I am waiting, yielded and still.

—Adelaide A. Pollard, "Have Thine Own Way, Lord" hymn

Questions for Discussion

1. What are some personal experiences you can share that have helped you understand the difficulty of reconciling the tension between divine sovereignty and human responsibility?

2. Has Jeremiah's sermon helped you to better clarify your theology on divine sovereignty and human responsibility or has it deepened the mystery?

3. How do you understand the point of no return—that point when a person hardens into a shape that is irredeemable? Is this perhaps what Jesus meant by the unforgiveable sin?

4. In witnessing to the lost, should we emphasize God's sovereignty or human responsibility? In ministry to the saints, which should we emphasize?

5. The Potter has a purpose for your life. Do you know what it is?

6. Describe an area of your life where being on the Potter's wheel is painful. Are you tempted to get off the wheel?

THE CAUSE AND CURE OF HOMESICKNESS

Jeremiah 29

All of us, to one degree or another, suffer from Destination Disease. The primary symptom of this malady is the persistent belief that "Happiness never will be found *here* where I presently am; it can only be found *over there*. When I get *there*, *then* I will be happy."

I remember well when I first became aware of my own battle with Destination Disease. I was in the first grade. When I looked down the hall and saw how big and how cool the fourth graders were, I realized I could never be happy in the first grade. My happiness would come only when I reached the elysian fields of fourth grade; however, once I arrived there, I realized I had been deceived. Fourth grade was no utopia. I discovered true happiness could be found only in middle school. But again, arriving at my coveted destination revealed I had been misled. I now learned that high school was the Shangri-La of happiness for which my soul longed. But once again, my hopes were dashed upon arrival. Rather than pausing, however, to consider whether my thinking might be wrong, I set my hopes on college…then marriage…then a career…then having a home full of children…then waiting for the day when the home would be empty of children. Where could happiness be found?

At 40 years of age, when I found myself thinking perhaps in retirement I would find true happiness, the absurdity of it all began to dawn on me. Destination Disease was consuming my life! I began to turn the sickness in my soul into a prayer: "Lord, where is true happiness to be found? Does it even exist? Where will I feel the release and relief of finally being home?" God answered the cry of my heart and began to teach me one of the most profound discoveries of my life.

The Lord showed me, through His Spirit and through His Word, that my disease was an ancient one. It is a genetic condition inherited from my distant ancestors, Adam and Eve. I had assumed my "dis-ease" was caused by the absence of happiness, but now I began to realize my problem was much deeper. It wasn't happiness that I sought—it was home! My problem was not Destination Disease but homesickness.

When Adam and Eve rebelled against God and ate the forbidden fruit, they were expelled from the Garden of Eden. In other words, the consequence of their decision to turn their backs on God was the loss of their true home. An angel with a flaming sword blocked the entrance so they could never return (Genesis 3:24). From that day forward, Adam and Eve and all their descendants have lived "in the land of Nod [Hebrew, *wandering*], east of Eden" (Genesis 4:16). There is a sense in which all human history can be described as mankind's wandering search, trying desperately to find the way back home. The Genesis story teaches us that the human condition is not just a struggle with sin; it is a struggle with homesickness. Our Destination Disease is in reality a deep awareness that we are aliens, wanderers, looking here and looking there, trying to find our way home. German philosophers called it *angst*. French existentialists called it *ennui*. Kierkegaard called it "sickness unto death." But perhaps the best word to describe the inner ache is *homesickness*.

Much of the world's great literature highlights this theme of homesickness as the defining reality of the human condition. For example, in *The Odyssey*, Homer describes the adventures of Ulysses after the Trojan War as he vainly tries to find his way back home to Ithaca. He is desperately homesick! One stop on the journey takes him to the island of the lotus-eaters. Here, travelers are "cured" of their homesickness by eating a plant that causes them to forget their true home. Ulysses rightly discerns that eating the lotus plant is the greatest danger his men have yet confronted, because if they forget their true home, all will be lost. The "cure" is infinitely worse than the disease!

In Tolkien's *The Lord of the Rings* trilogy, Frodo Baggins and Sam Gamgee present powerful illustrations of homesickness. For three long volumes, these two Hobbits travel over Middle Earth, obediently following the call that drives them. But the inner ache within them is palpable as they long to return to their home in the Shire. Their homesickness is a recurring theme throughout the trilogy. Near the end of the saga, when they finally get back to the Shire, Frodo realizes "home" is not what he had imagined it would be. Even in the Shire, he *still* suffers a homesickness that does not go away. So, he boards a ship and sails away into the sunset to his true home.

"But," said Sam, as tears started in his eyes, "I thought you were going to enjoy the Shire, too, for years and years, after all you have done."

"So I thought too, once," said Frodo. "But I have been too deeply hurt, Sam. I tried to save the Shire, and it has been saved, but not

for me. It must often be so, Sam, when things are in danger: some-
one has to give them up, lose them, so that others may keep them."[7]

Once one begins to see homesickness as an essential reality of the human condition, one is much better prepared to understand the Book of Jeremiah. For every Jew, Jerusalem is home. This is the City of God and the definitive location for understanding the faith of Abraham, Moses, and David. At a much deeper level than Ithaca for Ulysses or the Shire for Frodo, Jerusalem is the center of the universe and the ultimate depiction of home for every Hebrew. But in Jeremiah's day, God's people are exiled from Jerusalem and taken as hostages to Babylon, where they are forced to live and work. Destination Disease is raging through the Jewish community like a plague because the people are sick with desire to return home to Jerusalem. Jeremiah writes them a letter that rocks their world and redefines their understanding of home. His words will rock your world too!

A Letter from Home

Jeremiah 29 is a letter from home. Composed in perhaps 590 BC, the prophet is writing from Jerusalem to a group of Jewish exiles some 800 miles away in Babylon. A few years prior to this, Nebuchadnezzar and his army had come and attacked Jerusalem. Although he did not destroy the city at this time, he took 3,000 of its inhabitants into captivity. One can easily imagine the angst and dis-ease of these Jewish men and women so far from home. The food is different. The language is strange. The future is uncertain. They are alienated from all that is familiar. They *are* aliens. All they can think about is home!

---

7. J. R. R. Tolkien, *The Return of the King* (Boston: Houghton, 1955), 1006.

No two cities on earth are more symbolic than the two cities mentioned in Jeremiah 29. Jerusalem (Jeru-shalom) is the city of peace. Captured and built up by King David, this city is the dwelling place of God Himself. The Temple is the place where God has sworn that His presence will abide forever! Babylon, on the other hand, is the epitome of evil. Previously, the city was identified with Babel (Genesis 11:1–9), a place associated with human arrogance and divine judgment. In the future, Babylon will be identified as the Great Prostitute (Revelation 17–18). In one great and final rebellion against God, the city will be destroyed, definitively and completely: "So will Babylon the great city be thrown down with violence, and will be found no more" (Revelation 18:21). The contrast between these two cities makes the reality of homesickness extremely poignant. Oh how the Jewish exiles long to go home to Jerusalem. Babylon is not their home!

God prompted Jeremiah to write a letter to the homesick exiles and send it by the hand of Elasah. But the message contained in this letter is not what the captives want to hear. False prophets are predicting a short stay in exile and a speedy return to Jerusalem. One of these preachers is a man named Hananiah. His preaching is popular among the exiles.

Thus says the LORD of hosts, the God of Israel: I have broken the yoke of the king of Babylon. Within two years I will bring back to this place all the vessels of the LORD's house, which Nebuchadnezzar king of Babylon took away from this place and carried to Babylon. I will also bring back to this place Jeconiah the son of Jehoiakim, king of Judah, and all the exiles from Judah who went to Babylon, declares the LORD, for I will break the yoke of the king of Babylon. (Jeremiah 28:2–4)

This is just the message the exiles want to hear! How it must have brought comfort and peace to those suffering from homesickness. How the pews of churches where this message was preached must have been filled with eager listeners. How worship experiences that promoted the message of a speedy return must have caused worshipers to raise their hands in ecstatic praise. But from Jeremiah's perspective there is just one problem: the message is not true! In his letter, Jeremiah speaks words that must have sounded harsh and even cruel:

Thus says the LORD of hosts, the God of Israel, to all the exiles whom I have sent into exile from Jerusalem to Babylon: Build houses and live in them; plant gardens and eat their produce. Take wives and have sons and daughters; take wives for your sons, and give your daughters in marriage, that they may bear sons and daughters; multiply there, and do not decrease. But seek the welfare [shalom] of the city where I have sent you into exile, and pray to the LORD on its behalf, for in its welfare [shalom] you will find your welfare [shalom]. For thus says the LORD of hosts, the God of Israel: Do not let your prophets and your diviners who are among you deceive you, and do not listen to the dreams that they dream, for it is a lie that they are prophesying to you in my name; I did not send them, declares the LORD. For thus says the LORD, When seventy years are completed for Babylon, I will visit you, and I will fulfill to you my promise and bring you back to this place. For I know the plans I have for you, declares the LORD, plans for welfare [shalom] and not for evil, to give you a future and a hope. Then you will call upon me and come and pray to me, and I will hear you. You will seek me and find me, when you seek me with all your heart. I will be found by you, declares the LORD, and I will restore your fortunes and gather you from all

*the nations and all the places where I have driven you, declares
the LORD, and I will bring you back to the place from which I
sent you into exile.* (Jeremiah 29:4–14)

LIFE IN EXILE

Although Jeremiah's letter is not what the exiles in Babylon want
to hear, it is nevertheless full of practical admonitions for those who
find themselves far from their true home.

What Exiles Need to Remember

Imagine how living in Babylon could cause the people from
Jerusalem to forget their uniqueness. As they begin to eat the food,
speak the language, and practice the customs of the culture, it would
be easy for them to think they belonged to the city where they lived.
Jeremiah's letter is a bold reminder that for the people of God, our
location does not determine our citizenship. We may live in Babylon,
but we are not Babylonians! "Our citizenship is in heaven, and from
it we await a Savior, the Lord Jesus Christ" (Philippians 3:20).

The Jews in Jeremiah's day believed it was Nebuchadnezzar who
had put them in Babylon because of his imperialistic agenda. The
letter reminds them that it is the Lord Himself who placed them
there because of their sin. Babylon is the chosen location where God's
people learn to repent and be cleansed of their sins so the image of
God can be restored fully in them. In Babylon we remember who we
are and what we can become!

What Exiles Need to Do

Don't expect a quick deliverance! The Israelites' stay in Babylon will not be two years, but 70: a human lifetime. They are told to settle down, build houses, plant gardens, start families, and have children and grandchildren. As strange as it may sound, God tells His people to seek the well-being of Babylon! They are to pray for God's shalom to come into this evil city because their well-being is tied to Babylon's well-being. Amazingly, God loves the Babylonians even as He loves the Jews. So, He wants His people to live as testimonies of grace in a world of sin, as beacons of light in a city of darkness.

So, choose your prophets carefully! Jeremiah is bold to call *by name* those preachers of his day who were promoting lies and deceptions: Hananiah (Jeremiah 28:1–17), Ahab and Zedekiah (Jeremiah 29:21–23) and Shemaiah (Jeremiah 29:24–32). Stay away from false prophets! Don't go to their churches, don't read their books, and don't listen to their radio programs. Although they are preaching what you *want* to hear, they are not preaching what you *need* to know! When you live in Babylon, you can't be too careful about the voices you heed and the books you read. Choose your preachers carefully. Those who preach a short exile and a quick fix of health, wealth, and happiness are preaching lies! Such a "prosperity gospel" offers false comfort and false assurance. It announces a gospel that cannot save. Stay away from such teachings.

Do not listen to the words of the prophets who prophesy to you, filling you with vain hopes. They speak visions of their own minds, not from the mouth of the LORD. They say continually to those who despise the word of the LORD, 'It shall be well with you'; and to everyone who stubbornly follows his own heart, they say, 'No disaster shall come upon you'. …I did not send the prophets, yet they ran; I did not speak to them, yet they prophesied. But if they had stood in my council, then they would have proclaimed my words to my people. (Jeremiah 23:16–17, 21–22)

What Exiles Need to Believe

Believing in God and His promises may be difficult when you live in Jerusalem, but when you find yourself in Babylon, it is impossible without divine enabling! In Babylon, it is easy to conclude that God has abandoned you and that His promises are not true. Jeremiah's letter calls the people of God to put their trust in the Lord while living in a wicked city surrounded by paganism, secularism, atheism, agnosticism, and hedonism. Babylon is precisely the place where faith becomes *faith*! In Babylon, put your faith in God!

- Believe that He will take you home—in 70 years!
- Believe that He has good, not evil, plans for you!
- Believe that He is preparing for you a future and a hope!
- Believe that He will be found when you seek Him with all your heart—even in Babylon!
- Believe that one day He will restore your fortunes!

What Exiles Need to Know

In Babylon, it is easy to long for the "good ole' days" back in Jerusalem when everything was great and everyone was happy. But in Jeremiah's day, Jerusalem was filled with evil, unbelieving men and women who "did not pay attention to [God's] words" (Jeremiah 29:19). There is no shalom in Jeru-shalom! The citizens of Jerusalem are about to be consumed by sword, famine, and pestilence (Jeremiah 29:17). God's people are safer in Babylon than in Jerusalem!

Your prosperity, safety, and joy have nothing to do with your geographic location and everything to do with your spiritual condition. If you trust in the Lord and obey His commands, all will be well for you ultimately—even in Babylon. If you continue to live in rebellion and sin, judgment and wrath will fall upon you—even in Jerusalem.

You're Not Home Yet!

Few passages of Scripture speak more poignantly of homesickness than Psalm 137. Written by one who knew firsthand the bitterness of exile, this plaintive song recounts the struggle of a citizen of Jerusalem who was forced to live in Babylon.

> *By the waters of Babylon,*
> > *there we sat down and wept,*
> > *when we remembered Zion.*
> *On the willows there*
> > *we hung up our lyres.*
> *For there our captors*
> > *required of us songs,*
> *and our tormentors, mirth, saying,*
> > *"Sing us one of the songs of Zion!"*
> *How shall we sing the LORD's song*
> > *in a foreign land?*
> *If I forget you, O Jerusalem,*
> > *let my right hand forget its skill!*
> *Let my tongue stick to the roof of my mouth,*
> *if I do not remember you,*
> *If I do not set Jerusalem*
> > *above my highest joy!* (Psalm 137:1–6)

Perhaps the greatest challenge of the Christian walk is learning how to sing the Lord's song in a foreign land (Babylon). We must find the grace to live out the reality of our dual citizenship: citizens of Jerusalem, yet called to live as temporary residents in Babylon. Living with homesickness is a good disease to have! Don't eat the lotus plants that cause you to forget who you truly are and where your homeland truly is. Stop complaining of your location and seek the welfare (shalom) of that "city" where God has sent you into exile. In its welfare you will find your own welfare. Bloom where you are planted. Choose your pastors and preachers carefully. Don't fall for the kind of "prosperity gospel" that promises health, wealth, and happiness tomorrow. Realize that it may take 70 years for you to finally arrive home. So believe the promises of God and seek Him with all your heart. He will be found—even in Babylon!

Creatures are not born with desires unless satisfaction for those desires exists. A baby feels hunger: well, there is such a thing as food. A duckling wants to swim: well, there is such a thing as water. Men feel sexual desire: well, there is such a thing as sex. If I find in myself a desire which no experience in this world can satisfy, the most probable explanation is that I was made for another world.[8]

---

8. C. S. Lewis. *Mere Christianity* (New York: Harper, 2001), 136–137.

Questions for Discussion

1. Describe a time in your life when you were homesick. What was it like?

2. Have you ever gone "home" and then discovered it wasn't what you anticipated and it didn't feel like home?

3. Does "homesickness" seem like an apt description of the human condition? Could this influence the way you witness and share the gospel with those who are lost?

4. Describe what it means to you personally to "sing the Lord's song in a foreign land." Are you able to sing, or have you hung up your harp?

5. Why did our grandparents sing so much about heaven? Why does this generation sing so little about heaven?

6. Describe what it means to "eat the lotus plant" today?

7. How would you explain what it means to have dual citizenship?

THE BOOK OF CONSOLATION

Jeremiah 30—33

Earlier we noted that Jeremiah's job description was "to pluck up and to break down, to destroy and to overthrow, to build and to plant" (Jeremiah 1:10). Four verbs indicate how the prophet is to deal with the problem; two verbs point to how he is to deal with the solution. Most of Jeremiah's prophetic ministry is an illustration of the first four verbs. Because of Judah's willful disobedience and obstinate unbelief, God is sending judgment upon the sinful nation, uprooting and destroying them. Like a woeful litany, this theme of coming wrath is repeated over and over through most of the 52 chapters of the book. However, right in the middle of the book, four chapters focus on God's ultimate purpose "to build and to plant." This is the prophetic solution to Judah's sin and rebellion!

And it shall come to pass that as I have watched over them to pluck up and break down, to overthrow, destroy, and bring harm, so I will watch over them to build and to plant, declares the LORD. (Jeremiah 31:28)

Often called *The Book of Consolation*, chapters 30—33 form a dramatic contrast to the rest of the book:

Chapters 1—29 and 34—52	Chapters 30—33
Judgment and wrath on Judah	Grace and salvation on Judah
God plucks up, breaks down, destroys, and overthrows	God builds and plants
The present is terrible (things fall apart)	The future is glorious (the center can hold)
Humans are the primary actors	God is the primary actor ("I will…")
The wages of sin is death…	But the gift of God is eternal life (Romans 6:23)
Where sin abounded…	Grace abounded even more (Romans 5:20)

GOD STEPS IN

Throughout most of the Book of Jeremiah, one is tempted to ask, "Where is God?" As things fall apart, it seems that God is either absent or His presence is manifested only in His terrible wrath and judgment. In these four chapters, God steps into the picture. He is in full control and He has come to forgive, to restore, and to bless. The most obvious characteristic of this beautiful passage is the repeated statement made by God Himself that He will act for the salvation of His people. Over 60 times God says, "I will." Here are just 28 of them:

I will restore the fortunes of My people. (30:3, 18; 32:44; 33:7, 11, 26)

I will bring you back to the land. (30:3; 32:37)

I will break the yoke of the king of Babylon. (30:8)

I will burst your bonds. (30:8)

I will save you. (30:10)

I will make a full end of other nations but not of you. (30:11)

I will restore health to you and heal you. (30:17)

FIRE IN HIS BONES

I will multiply you and honor you. (30:19)

I will punish those who oppress you. (30:20)

I will be your God and you will be My people. (30:22; 31:33; 32:38)

I will build you and you shall be built. (31:4)

I will gather you from all the places I scattered you. (31:8–9; 32:37)

I will turn your mourning to joy and your sorrow to gladness. (31:13)

I will satisfy the weary soul and replenish the languishing soul. (31:25)

I will build you up and plant you. (31:28)

I will make a new and everlasting covenant with you. (31:31; 32:40)

I will put my law within you and write it on your hearts. (31:33)

I will forgive your iniquity and remember your sin no more. (31:34)

I will make you dwell in safety. (32:37)

I will give you one heart and one way. (32:39)

I will not turn away from doing good to you. (32:40)

I will rejoice in doing good to you. (32:41)

I will bring upon you all the good I promised you. (32:42)

I will answer you when you call to Me. (33:3)

I will show you great and hidden things you have not known. (33:3)

I will bring healing to this city and make it prosperous and secure. (33:6)

I will cleanse you from all the guilt of your sin. (33:8)

I will cause a righteous Branch to spring up for David. (33:15–16)

The consolation the prophet brings to Judah is that "behold, days are coming" (30:3) when God Himself will step onto the stage of human history and right every wrong and offer forgiveness for every sin. Every promise He has ever made will be gloriously fulfilled. Therefore, put your hope in Him and wait for Him to come in saving power.

WHAT GOD IS GOING TO DO

Although God is going to save Judah and restore her fortunes, He in no way minimizes the seriousness of her sin. The first chapter of the Book of Consolation says what at first sounds like a contradiction: Israel's sinful condition is incurable and beyond hope—yet God will cure her anyway! There is hope in the midst of Israel's hopelessness!

> *Thus says the LORD:*
> *Your hurt is incurable,*
> > *and your wound is grievous.*
> *There is none to uphold your cause,*
> > *no medicine for your wound,*
> > *no healing for you…*
>
> *Why do you cry out over your hurt?*
> > *Your pain is incurable.*
> *Because your guilt is great,*
> > *because your sins are flagrant,*
> > *I have done these things to you.*
> *Therefore all who devour you shall be devoured,*
> > *and all your foes, every one of them, shall go into captivity;*
> *those who plunder you shall be plundered,*
> > *and all who prey on you I will make a prey.*
> *For I will restore health to you,*
> > *and your wounds I will heal,*
> *declares the LORD.* (Jeremiah 30:12–13, 15–17)

How can God say, "Your hurt is incurable" in one verse and in the next verse say, "Your wounds I will heal"? Part of the answer is found in the heart of God, where infinite justice and infinite mercy reside together. As any parent knows so well, when you love your children and want what is right and true for them, you sometimes say things that sound contradictory. At times you tend more toward justice and other times you tend more toward mercy. Such is the paradoxical reality of our heavenly Father. His truth demands justice against our sins. Yet His mercy demands grace. Our sickness is incurable; and yet God can cure it. Our situation is hopeless; and yet God promises hope for our future. Both realities are gloriously true. This may not make sense today, but "in the latter days you will understand this" (Jeremiah 30:24).

What is God doing? He is devising a way to cure the incurable, to redeem the irredeemable, to forgive the unforgiveable, and to bring hope to the hopeless! This may seem impossible, but nothing is too hard for God (Jeremiah 32:17).

Centuries after Jeremiah, when God sent His Son to die on a cross for the sins of the world, we began to understand how justice and grace can work together so the salvation of sinners becomes possible. But in Jeremiah's day, He simply asks His people to trust Him and believe in the promises—even when it doesn't make sense: *"Call to me and I will answer you, and will tell you great and hidden things that you have not known"* (Jeremiah 33:3).

> *What is God doing? He is devising a way to cure the incurable, to redeem the irredeemable, to forgive the unforgiveable, and to bring hope to the hopeless!*

Why and How God Is Going to Do It

But *why* would God even want to redeem and restore such ungrateful rebels? What possible motivation could be at work to cause a holy God to lavish such blessings on such a wicked nation? Chapter 31 gives us the answer:

> *I have loved you with an everlasting love;*
> *therefore I have continued my faithfulness to you.* (31:3)

> *I am a father to Israel,*
> *and Ephraim is my firstborn.* (31:9)

> *Is Ephraim my dear son?*
> *Is he my darling child?*
> *For as often as I speak against him,*
> *I do remember him still.*
> *Therefore my heart yearns for him;*
> *I will surely have mercy on him,*
> *declares the* Lord. (31:20)

For some reason known only to God, the Lord loves the people of Israel. He has chosen them from among all the nations of the earth and has made a covenant of love with them. Israel is not loved because of any merit in her. In fact, she's done nothing to deserve such blessings. The explanation for such matchless love is not to be found in the beloved but in the lover. It is God's nature to love. With God, love is not just something He does; it is who He is: God is love (1 John 4:16); But God shows His love for us in that while we were still sinners, Christ died for us (Romans 5:8). God loves us not because we are loveable but because it is His nature to love. God is a Father (Jeremiah 31:9) who loves His children with self-giving love. He loves us because He loves us.

Chapter 31

Behold, I will bring them from the north country
*   and gather them from the farthest parts of the earth,*
among them the blind and the lame,
*   the pregnant woman and she who is in labor, together;*
*   a great company, they shall return here.* (31:8)

They shall come and sing aloud on the height of Zion,
*   and they shall be radiant over the goodness of the LORD,*
over the grain, the wine, and the oil,
*   and over the young of the flock and the herd;*
their life shall be like a watered garden,
*   and they shall languish no more.*
Then shall the young women rejoice in the dance,
*   and the young men and the old shall be merry.*
I will turn their mourning into joy;
*   I will comfort them, and give them gladness for sorrow.*
I will feast the soul of the priests with abundance,
*   and my people shall be satisfied with my goodness,*
declares the LORD (31:12–14).

I will satisfy the weary soul, and every languishing soul I will
replenish (31:25).

Thus says the LORD,
who gives the sun for light by day
*   and the fixed order of the moon and the stars for light by night,*
who stirs up the sea so that its waves roar—
*   the LORD of hosts is his name:*
"If this fixed order departs
*   from before me, declares the LORD,*

then shall the offspring of Israel cease
    from being a nation before me forever."

Thus says the LORD:
"If the heavens above can be measured,
    and the foundations of the earth below can be explored,
then I will cast off all the offspring of Israel
    for all that they have done,
declares the LORD" (35–37).

But *how* will God do this? What method, what means will He use to restore a relationship broken by sin? And how can we be sure that when the captives return to Zion they won't fall once again into sin? Can even God redeem the irredeemable and cure the incurable? Chapter 31 of Jeremiah responds to that question with a twofold answer.

God Is Doing Something New

God promises He is doing something entirely new; something unprecedented. "The LORD has created a new thing on the earth: a woman encircles a man" (31:22). The word created points to a work that only God could do. While men can "make" things, only God can "create." The "new thing" seems to be a reversal of the natural order. A woman "encircles" (surrounds, encompasses, protects) a man. Obviously, the prophet wants us to understand that God is doing something unusual, something that never has been done before!

Most modern scholars understand this passage to mean that God is working things so Israel, God's bride, will begin to initiate a relationship with her husband (God). In the past, God has been the initiator, but now, because of redemption, Israel will take the lead and "surround" (embrace, encircle) her lover. While this is a possible interpretation, I am inclined to take the more historic understanding held by men such as Augustine, Jerome, and Matthew Henry. In this view, God is speaking about the incarnation and the virgin birth. The "new thing" God has done "on the earth" is for a woman (a virgin) to surround (encircle, carry in her womb) a man (the God-man, Jesus Christ). Jeremiah seems to be saying that the only way Judah can be redeemed is if God Himself does something unprecedented and "new." Israel's sickness and lost condition is so absolute that unless God comes up with a plan that never has been tried before, her condition is hopeless!

The gospel announces this is exactly what God has done. He loved the world so much that He came Himself to live in a world where things fall apart. He arrived encircled in the womb of a virgin peasant girl named Mary. Who in their wildest dreams could have imagined such a story? God created a new thing on the earth. He came—through a woman!

The idea that Jeremiah is talking about the incarnation in this passage is further underscored by the fact that Matthew quotes from this chapter in his telling of the birth of Jesus (Matthew 2:16–18). When Herod sends soldiers to kill the baby boys in Bethlehem, Mary protects (surrounds, encircles, encompasses) the Son of God and saves His life. From Matthew's perspective, Jeremiah is prophesying events related to the birth of Jesus when he writes, *"A voice was heard in Ramah, weeping and loud lamentation, Rachel weeping for her children; she refused to be comforted, because they are no more"* (Matthew 2:18; see also Jeremiah 31:15).

God Is Making a New Covenant

Few passages in the Bible are more important than Jeremiah 31:31–34. It is not that the Old Covenant made at Mount Sinai is flawed, but simply that there are some things this covenant cannot do. Indeed, it was never designed to do them! The Old Covenant could convict of sin but it could not cleanse the heart. God built obsolescence into the Mosaic covenant (see Hebrews 8:13) so that He could complete His work of redemption by establishing a new and better covenant based on the death and resurrection of Jesus Christ (Hebrews 8:6–13; 9:13–15; 10:9).

> *Behold, the days are coming, declares the LORD, when I will make a new covenant with the house of Israel and the house of Judah, not like the covenant that I made with their fathers on the day when I took them by the hand to bring them out of the land of Egypt, my covenant that they broke, though I was their husband, declares the LORD. For this is the covenant that I will make with the house of Israel after those days, declares the LORD: I will put my law within them, and I will write it on their hearts. And I will be their God, and they shall be my people. And no longer shall each one teach his neighbor and each his brother, saying, 'Know the LORD,' for they shall all know me, from the least of them to the greatest, declares the LORD. For I will forgive their iniquity, and I will remember their sin no more.* (Jeremiah 31:31–34)

These two covenants, the Old Covenant with Moses at Mount Sinai and the New Covenant with Jesus at Mount Calvary, are not just a description of Israel's history through time. They describe the journey disciples of Jesus typically take as they discover the unfolding reality of grace in their lives. The covenant at Sinai gets us started, assuring us of God's covenant love and promises. But without the deeper work the New Covenant makes possible, we risk wandering in the wilderness of spiritual mediocrity for the rest of our days. The two covenants represent two stages of the Christian life. Israel desperately needs to move from the Old Covenant to the New Covenant in Jeremiah's day, and making the same transition is what many lukewarm Christians desperately need to do today. Only as we experience the dynamic transformation promised in the New Covenant do we begin to understand the reality of Calvary and Pentecost in our lives. In these verses we see at least three ways the New Covenant is better than the Old Covenant.

First, the New Covenant makes possible *a new motivation*. The covenant established by Moses was written on tablets of stone. The motivation to keep it was often the fear of what might happen if one didn't! Such emphasis on outward conformity led to Phariseeism and legalism that by Jesus' day had become widespread.

The Old Covenant tends to communicate the idea that being a Christian is all about outward actions and behavior modification. The New Covenant, however, has a radically different approach. God says, "I will put my law [Hebrew, torah] within them, and I will write it on their hearts" (Jeremiah 31:33). People under the New Covenant obey God's ways not because they *have* to, but because they *want* to! Such an understanding of the gospel prompted Augustine to say, "Love God and do what you want." He was not promoting license to live in sin but was underscoring the fact that when someone really loves God, they naturally will desire to please Him by doing what He wants. The New Covenant makes possible a transformed heart so that obedience becomes a joy rather than a duty.

Second, the New Covenant makes possible *a new relationship*. The Old Covenant made it possible to have a relationship with God, but only a few knew Him face-to-face. Most only knew *about* God.

The New Covenant, however, makes it possible to know God in a personal and intimate way: "They shall all know me, from the least of them to the greatest" (Jeremiah 31:34). This intimate relationship with God is not just for spiritual giants and saints. It is for everyone, everywhere. When Jesus died, the veil in the Temple was torn in two so that now it is possible to enter boldly into the very presence of God (Matthew 27:51; Hebrews 4:16; 6:19; 10:19–22). The New Covenant is not the offer of a new religion but a new relationship!

Let not the wise man boast in his wisdom, let not the mighty man boast in his might, let not the rich man boast in his riches, but let him who boasts boast in this, that he understands and knows me, that I am the LORD. (Jeremiah 9:23–24)

Finally, the New Covenant makes possible *a new power*. The Old Covenant promised forgiveness for outward acts of sin but made no real provision for cleansing from the inward nature of sin. The New Covenant is God's promise to do more with sin than forgive it; He intends to break its power! Not only does God want to forgive our sinful deeds (Jeremiah 31:34), but He also longs to cleanse our sinful hearts: "I will cleanse them from all the guilt of their sin" (Jeremiah 33:8). Jesus Christ shed His blood to forgive our sinful actions and poured out His sanctifying Spirit to cleanse our sinful nature. Not only are the consequences of sin erased, but also the power of sin is broken! "If we confess our sins, he is faithful and just to forgive us our sins and to cleanse us from all unrighteousness" (1 John 1:9, emphases mine).

How God's Glorious Future Affects Us Today

In the light of God's amazing love for sinners and His readiness to make a New Covenant with people like us, how then should we live? What sort of people ought we to be? In Jeremiah's day, outward circumstances remain unchanged. Things are falling apart. Jerusalem is in ruins and God's people still live in Babylon. And so it is with us today. We hear the gospel but our circumstances generally remain the same. What difference do these promises of God make for people like us? Chapters 32—33 orient us to three primary responsibilities that we have as children of God to live out our lives today in the midst of a wicked and perverse generation.

Trust in God and His Promises

Believe in God even when you live in Babylon and life doesn't make sense. Let the promises for tomorrow change the way you live today! Even though the Babylonian army is laying siege to Jerusalem, God tells Jeremiah to buy a piece of property in Judah (32:1–15). What? The nation is about to be destroyed and the people sent into captivity. Is this any time to invest in real estate? But this act of obedience is the prophet's way to the promises of God. Although the nation goes into exile for 70 years and although Jeremiah himself dies in Egypt and never gets to enjoy the property he purchases, his action is a bold statement of faith: God's word is true even though outward circumstances may make you think just the opposite! Nothing is too hard for God (Jeremiah 32:17, 27).

> *God's word is true even though outward circumstances may make you think just the opposite!*

Pray, Pray, Pray

As things are falling apart all around Jeremiah, God invites him to pray: "Call to me and I will answer you, and will tell you great and hidden things that you have not known" (Jeremiah 33:3). We can survive and even thrive in desperate situations if we know how to talk with God.

Keep Looking to Jesus

He came once, humble and riding on a donkey. He came to give His life as a ransom for sin. Only a few recognized who He was. But the next time He comes, He will be riding a horse prepared for battle. Every eye will see Him and He will judge the living and the dead and bring justice to the nations (Revelation 1:7; 19:11–16; 22:20). So keep watching the horizon. Perhaps He'll come today!

In those days and at that time I will cause a righteous Branch to spring up for David, and he shall execute justice and righteousness in the land. In those days Judah will be saved, and Jerusalem will dwell securely. And this is the name by which it will be called: "The LORD is our righteousness." (Jeremiah 33:15–16)

Questions for Discussion

1. Why does God say Israel's sin is "incurable" and then announce that He will heal them?

2. How do you think God can forgive sin without compromising His justice? Discuss.

3. What is the difference between forgiveness and cleansing? How does the gospel provide for both? Are these distinct experiences in our journey?

4. When it comes to salvation, what is God's part? What is our part?

5. At times, it seems that some of God's people fell from grace and were lost forever (the ten northern tribes). At other times, it seems that God will let no one go—ever! How do you understand the security of the believer? Has this study changed your belief in some way or perhaps strengthened it?

6. Is anything too hard for God? Can He save sinners who don't want to be saved?

BARUCH THE MAGNIFICENT

Jeremiah 45

Someone once asked Leonard Bernstein, the legendary conductor of the New York Philharmonic, what was the most difficult instrument in the orchestra to play. Without hesitation the famous maestro responded, "Second fiddle."

It is not easy to serve in the shadow of someone else. It is difficult to play a role that is invisible, unnoticed, and unappreciated. It takes great grace to quietly work behind the scenes while someone else gets all the attention. Yet that is precisely what most of us are called to do! God asks only a few to serve at the center of the stage under the lights for all to see. Most of us are called to roles of humble, invisible service, making possible the ministries of those called to the center of public attention.

In this chapter, we examine the life of the man who played second fiddle to Jeremiah: Baruch Ben Neriah. Never heard of him? That's just the point. Although his ministry is almost completely invisible and many don't even recognize his name, we can safely say there never would have been a Jeremiah the prophet had it not been for Baruch the scribe. Indeed, he is the unsung hero of the entire book!

Four passages in the Book of Jeremiah give us a glimpse of the indispensable role played by Baruch. These cameo appearances help us to better understand what is involved in playing second fiddle in God's orchestra.

JEREMIAH 36:1–32

The text indicates that the events recorded in this chapter occur "in the fourth year of Jehoiakim" (36:1). Most scholars believe this would have been 605 BC. This year is of great significance in world history because it is when the Battle of Carchemish was fought (see 46:2). When the Babylonian army defeats the Assyrians and their ally, Egypt, at Carchemish, the balance of power in the Ancient Near East shifts and world history takes a new direction. Because tiny Judah had allied herself with Egypt, her fate is now sealed. The Babylonians will soon be heading her way to seek revenge on Judah for siding with their enemy.

Although this passage has much interesting information on how Scripture comes into being, our focus is not so much on the text as on the one who writes it: Baruch Ben Neriah. God tells Jeremiah to "take a scroll and write on it all the words that I have spoken to you" (36:2). In obedience, Jeremiah calls his secretary (scribe) Baruch who "wrote on a scroll at the dictation of Jeremiah all the words of the LORD that he had spoken to him" (36:4). This was state of the art technology for that day and writing such a scroll would have required many days of tedious labor. The message on this scroll is the prophetic announcement that the king of Babylon would soon come and destroy Jerusalem (36:29). The Lord hoped the shocking prophecy would cause the inhabitants of Jerusalem to repent (36:3). Indeed, if they did turn from their sins, God would turn from His wrath and the nation could be saved (Jeremiah 18:7–8). Not only is Baruch to serve as a scribe but also as a sort of substitute preacher:

Jeremiah ordered Baruch, saying, "I am banned from going to the house of the LORD, so you are to go, and on a day of fasting in the hearing of all the people in the LORD's house you shall read the words of the LORD from the scroll that you have written at my dictation…. And Baruch the son of Neriah did all that Jeremiah the prophet ordered him about reading from the scroll the words of the LORD in the LORD's house. (36:5–6, 8)

Some of the leaders in Jerusalem are so troubled by the message they call for a private interview with Baruch, asking him to clarify the origin of the message he has just read. Baruch explains that the prophet Jeremiah "dictated all these words to me, while I wrote them with ink on the scroll" (36:18). Telling Baruch to take Jeremiah and go and hide, the leaders then report these matters to king Jehoiakim. A man named Jehudi reads the scroll to the king. But rather than leading him to repentance, the message causes the king to stiffen his neck and harden his heart in rebellion:

It was the ninth month, and the king was sitting in the winter house, and there was a fire burning in the fire pot before him. As Jehudi read three or four columns, the king would cut them off with a knife and throw them into the fire in the fire pot, until the entire scroll was consumed in the fire that was in the fire pot. Yet neither the king nor any of his servants who heard all these words was afraid, nor did they tear their garments. Even when Elnathan and Delaiah and Gemariah urged the king not to burn the scroll, he would not listen to them. And the king commanded Jerahmeel…and Seraiah…and Shelemiah…to seize Baruch the secretary and Jeremiah the prophet, but the LORD hid them. (36:22–26)

What a contrast this is to the way the king's father, Josiah, had responded 17 years earlier when a lost scroll containing God's Word had been discovered in the Temple and read to him (2 Kings 22:8–13). In that situation, King Josiah led the nation in repentance and the Lord sent a season of revival to the land.

We can only imagine the dismay and discouragement Jeremiah and Baruch must have been feeling as God's Word went up in flames! All their labor of dictation and writing was in vain, and now Israel's hope of salvation was gone as well. But although the prophet and his secretary may have felt all was lost, God didn't.

> *After the king had burned the scroll with the words that Baruch wrote at Jeremiah's dictation, the word of the LORD came to Jeremiah: "Take another scroll and write on it all the former words that were in the first scroll.... Then Jeremiah took another scroll and gave it to Baruch the scribe, the son of Neriah, who wrote on it at the dictation of Jeremiah all the words of the scroll that Jehoiakim king of Judah had burned in the fire. And many similar words were added to them.* (36:27–28, 32)

The prophet and the scribe sit down together and patiently go through the process all over again. Imagine what it must have meant to Jeremiah to have at his side such a devoted, competent, loyal, steadfast, and courageous friend. Without the assistance of this second-fiddle player, we never would have heard the "music" Jeremiah was sent to play.

JEREMIAH 32:1–5

Although this passage is from an earlier chapter, the events described actually occur later than those we just examined in chapter 36. It is during the tenth year of Zedekiah king of Judah (about 587 BC), at the time when "the army of the king of Babylon was besieging Jerusalem, and Jeremiah the prophet was shut up in the court of the guard that was in the palace of the king of Judah" (32:2) that God gives Jeremiah a strange command:

> *The word of the* LORD *came to me. Behold, Hanamel the son of Shallum your uncle will come to you and say, "Buy my field that is at Anathoth, for the right of redemption by purchase is yours."…*
> *And I bought the field at Anathoth from Hanamel my cousin, and weighed out the money to him, seventeen shekels of silver. I signed the deed, sealed it, got witnesses, and weighed the money on scales…. And I gave the deed of purchase to Baruch the son of Neriah…. I charged Baruch in their presence, saying, "Thus says the* LORD *of hosts, the God of Israel: Take these deeds, both this sealed deed of purchase and this open deed, and put them in an earthenware vessel, that they may last for a long time. For thus says the* LORD *of hosts, the God of Israel: Houses and fields and vineyards shall again be bought in this land."* (32:6–7, 9–15)

This is remarkable. The city is under siege and about to be destroyed, Jeremiah is in prison, and the inhabitants of Jerusalem are about to be taken into exile, yet God tells the prophet to invest in Judean real estate! The prophet's action is a public statement of faith in the promises of God. Yes, Jerusalem will be destroyed and the people sent into exile for many years. But they'll be back. Judean real estate is still a good investment! It is noteworthy that when Jeremiah needs someone trustworthy to be the executor of his estate, he chooses his faithful friend, Baruch Ben Neriah.

JEREMIAH 43:1–7

This passage describes a time after the destruction of Jerusalem (about 586 BC). The Babylonians have placed a puppet ruler named Gedaliah on the throne of Judah, but he is murdered (see chapter 41). Everyone knows the Babylonians will soon come back to deal with the situation. Panic grips the hearts of the remaining inhabitants of Jerusalem as they contemplate the best course of action. Many decide the best thing is to flee to Egypt for safety. The Lord speaks through Jeremiah, however, warning against such a decision.

> *If you will remain in this land, then I will build you up and not pull you down; I will plant you, and not pluck you up; for I relent of the disaster that I did to you. Do not fear the king of Babylon….for I am with you, to save you…. But if you say, "We will not remain in this land," disobeying the voice of the LORD your God and saying, "No, we will go to the land of Egypt, where we shall not see war or hear the sound of the trumpet or be hungry for bread, and we shall dwell there," then hear the word of the LORD, O remnant of Judah. Thus says the LORD of hosts, the God of Israel: If you set your faces to enter Egypt and go to live there, then the sword that you fear shall overtake you there in the land of Egypt, and the famine of which you are afraid shall follow close after you to Egypt, and there you shall die. …"Do not go to Egypt." Know for a certainty that I have warned you this day.* (42:10–16, 19)

The leaders in Jerusalem refuse to listen to the prophet's message and most pack their bags and head south to Egypt. With arrogance these leaders accuse God's prophet of telling lies. Perhaps most shocking of all, they accuse Baruch of being the real source of what they believe is Jeremiah's false message!

You are telling a lie. The LORD *our God did not send you to say,
"Do not go to Egypt to live there," but Baruch the son of Neriah
has set you against us, to deliver us into the hand of the Chaldeans, that they may kill us or take us into exile in Babylon."*
(43:2–3)

The result of these tragic events is that Jeremiah (now about 70
years of age) and Baruch are forced to accompany the people as they
head off to Egypt. This is the last picture we have of Jeremiah the
prophet: an old man forced against his will to travel to Egypt, where
he ultimately will die. And with him to the very end is his faithful
friend, Baruch the son of Neriah.

JEREMIAH 45:1–5

A final passage that mentions the scribe Baruch is actually a short
sermon. Jeremiah is the preacher and Baruch is the congregation!
This passage reveals the true secret of Baruch's greatness more than
any other passage. Apparently, Baruch struggled at times with his
calling to play second fiddle. There were moments when he wanted
to be up front, playing first-chair violin!

For one thing, he came from a prominent family. His brother
Seraiah was the king's quartermaster (chief of staff) (Jeremiah
51:59) and his grandfather, Mahseiah, may have been a governor of
Jerusalem (2 Chronicles 34:8). For another thing, Baruch was highly
educated and had exceptional talents. Few men in that day had the
ability to write and record messages on scrolls. Clearly, Baruch would
have had other career options to consider. Becoming secretary to
the king would have looked good on his résumé. Being secretary
to a fire-breathing, pulpit-pounding prophet of doom was hardly

the path to career advancement. As Jeremiah's ministry continued to encounter resistance and rejection, there must have been moments when Baruch wondered if he had made the right choice. Thus, the sermon Jeremiah preaches to his secretary is poignant and powerful.

The word that Jeremiah the prophet spoke to Baruch the son of Neriah, when he wrote these words in a book at the dictation of Jeremiah, in the fourth year of Jehoiakim the son of Josiah, king of Judah: "Thus says the LORD, the God of Israel, to you, O Baruch: You said, 'Woe is me! For the LORD has added sorrow to my pain. I am weary with my groaning, and I find no rest.' Thus shall you say to him, Thus says the LORD: Behold, what I have built I am breaking down, and what I have planted I am plucking up—that is, the whole land. And do you seek great things for yourself? Seek them not, for behold, I am bringing disaster upon all flesh, declares the LORD. But I will give you your life as a prize of war in all places to which you may go." (45:1–5)

It must have been difficult to be the sidekick to a prophet of doom. At times Baruch must have felt he'd had enough. "Woe is me! I'm weary with my groaning, and I find no rest." There must have been other times when Baruch wished he could play first fiddle. He had his own thoughts and opinions about God's will and current events. He was educated and gifted. Why did he have to be a scribe for someone else? Apparently, sometimes Baruch chafed at this calling to work in the shadow of someone else. On occasion Baruch wanted to live his own life and become great himself.

The sermon Baruch hears is not a pleasant one. Jeremiah does not thank him for all the faithful service he has performed. Basically, God's message to Baruch is this: "Do you seek great things for yourself? Get over it! You are called to be secretary to Jeremiah, whom I have called to be a prophet. So just do your job and find your contentment in it!" God shows little sympathy toward those who resist the role He has chosen for them to fill. And yet God wants to reward Baruch. He recognizes the difficulty of the job he's been assigned and so gives him a beautiful promise: "I will give you your life as a prize of war in all places to which you may go."

BARUCH THE MAGNIFICENT

In the sixth century BC, Jeremiah is a bright and shining light, like the sun. Baruch is much smaller, like the moon, always living in the shadow of the prophet and reflecting his brilliance. Sometimes the moon actually blots out the sun. A solar eclipse occurs when the tiny moon comes between the earth and the sun in such a way as to block it from sight. In these final paragraphs, I want to create a similar situation by allowing Baruch to eclipse Jeremiah. We typically read the Book of Jeremiah and conclude that nothing is more brilliant than the prophet and his message; however, there would be no Jeremiah without Baruch. We see at least five magnificent qualities in the life of Baruch that make him a noble saint of God and that each of us should aspire to emulate.

Discernment

Jeremiah is not the only preacher in town. As we have seen, other prophets are present, and frankly, they are much more popular. But Baruch is able to distinguish truth from error, light from darkness, and wheat from chaff. At some point he makes a conscious choice to identify with a preacher who is unpopular and a message that is detested. Identifying with Jeremiah puts an end to any hopes Baruch may have had for career advancement. He chooses to cast his lot with Jeremiah, not because it is the popular thing to do but because it is the right thing to do. The real challenge of playing second fiddle is not being second but making sure we are playing in the right orchestra. There is no virtue in being the secretary to a false prophet! We see the magnificence of Baruch not in the fact that he is a humble servant but in the fact that he is a humble servant to a man of God.

Most people imagine Frodo is the hero in *The Lord of the Rings* trilogy. But think again. Perhaps Sam Gamgee is better qualified to wear such a title. Although Frodo is the one called to carry the ring and save Middle Earth from destruction, Sam enables Frodo to carry out his mission: helping him, encouraging him, and protecting him. At one crucial moment near the end of their journey, Frodo is so weary he wants to quit. He asks Sam to carry the ring the rest of the way without him. But Sam knows he isn't the ring bearer and never can be. In so many words he says to Frodo, "I can't carry the ring; but I can carry you!" Sam then lifts his friend onto his shoulders and carries him the rest of the way (see Vol. III *Return of the King*, 919). Frodo succeeds in his mission only because of Sam. The same could be said of Jeremiah and Baruch. Every time Jeremiah wants to quit, Baruch the Magnificent is at his side to support, to encourage, to protect, and to love.

Contentment in Being Invisible

Baruch learns to work in the shadows, behind the scenes. Most of what he does is unnoticed and unappreciated. Most people don't even know his name. And yet without him two books of the Bible would be missing (Jeremiah and Lamentations). Although he struggles at times with his calling and aspires to do great things himself, he finally learns contentment in being invisible.

At some point in David's life, he too had to learn contentment with a calling from God that seemed to confine him to hidden places where no one noticed him or even cared. In such a moment, he wrote these words:

> O LORD, my heart is not lifted up;
>   my eyes are not raised too high;
> I do not occupy myself with things
>   too great and too marvelous for me.
> But I have calmed and quieted my soul,
>   like a weaned child with its mother;
>   like a weaned child is my soul within me.
> O Israel, hope in the LORD
>   from this time forth and forevermore. (Psalm 131:1–3)

JOY IN SERVING

Baruch finds his identity, his mission, and ultimately his joy in serving someone else. Only those who are secure in their own worth and identity as a child of God find joy in serving. Jesus washed the dirty feet of His disciples (John 13:3–5) only because He knew "the Father had given all things into his hands, and that he had come from God and was going back to God." Only when we have the mind of Christ are we able to "do nothing from selfish ambition or conceit, but in humility count others more significant than [ourselves]" (Philippians 2:3). In His self-giving love for others, Jesus models a type of leadership and greatness the world has never seen. He says,

> "You know that those who are considered rulers of the Gentiles lord it over them, and their great ones exercise authority over

them. But it shall not be so among you. But whoever would be great among you must be your servant, and whoever would be first among you must be slave of all. For even the Son of Man came not to be served but to serve, and to give his life as a ransom for many." (Mark 10:42–45)

The Beauty of Humility

Although Baruch has a good education, is multitalented, and has various opportunities to advance his own career, he finds his ultimate place of service in promoting someone else. As C. S. Lewis pointed out in his classic book *Mere Christianity*, humility is not thinking badly of yourself; it is not thinking of yourself at all (see chapter, "The Great Sin"). True humility has a distinctive and enticingly sweet aroma. Baruch found greatness when he stopped looking for it: "And do you seek great things for yourself? Seek them not" (Jeremiah 45:5). Speaking to the believers in Corinth who boasted of their spiritual gifts and abilities, Paul had this to say: "*This 'knowledge' puffs up, but love builds up. If anyone imagines that he knows something, he does not yet know as he ought to know"* (1 Corinthians 8:1–3).

Agape Love and the Power of Self-Forgetfulness

No one can be magnificent like Baruch until the agape love of God has been poured into his or her heart (Romans 5:5). This kind of life demands a supernatural explanation. We can give our lives for others only because Christ has given His life for us. When the Spirit of Christ fills us, then we, like Baruch, begin to find our greatest joy in pouring out our lives for someone else.

1. What does it mean to play "second fiddle"? Share your thoughts, making it personal.

2. Do you identify more with Jeremiah and his call to public ministry or with Baruch and his call to invisible service? Discuss the relationship between the one being served (Jeremiah) and the one who serves (Baruch).

3. Think of those you know who are invisible and unnoticed and yet play an indispensable role. What can you do to express appreciation and encourage them in their work?

4. When you find yourself playing second fiddle, do you ever complain, "Woe is me; I am weary with my groaning"?

5. Are you seeking great things for yourself?

6. Look again at the five magnificent qualities we see in Baruch's life: discernment, invisibility, joy in serving, humility, and agape love. Which trait is weakest in your life? What do you intend to do about it?

SINGING THE BLUES

The Book of Lamentations

Max Lucado tells a delightful story that serves as a great introduction to the Book of Lamentations:

Chippie the parakeet never saw it coming. One second he was peacefully perched in his cage. The next he was sucked in, washed up, and blown over. The problems began when Chippie's owner decided to clean Chippie's cage with a vacuum cleaner. She removed the attachment from the end of the hose and stuck it in the cage. The phone rang, and she turned to pick it up. She'd barely said "hello" when "sssopp!" Chippie got sucked in. The bird owner gasped, and put down the phone, turned off the vacuum, and opened the bag. There was Chippie—still alive, but stunned. Since the bird was covered with dust and soot, she grabbed him and raced to the bathroom, turned on the faucet, and held Chippie under the running water. Then, realizing that Chippie was soaked and shivering, she did what any compassionate owner would do…she reached for the hair dryer and blasted the pet with hot air. Poor Chippie never knew what hit him. A few days after the trauma, the reporter who'd initially written about the event contacted Chippie's owner to see how the bird was recovering. "Well," she replied, "Chippie doesn't sing much anymore—he just sits and stares." [9]

Have you ever felt like Chippie? When affliction and hardship comes in like a flood, we sometimes survive the crisis but lose our ability to sing. This final chapter will help us see how Jeremiah and some of his compatriots learn to respond when things in Jerusalem fall apart. Amazingly, although they lose almost everything else, they don't lose their song!

Things Fall Apart

Jeremiah's prophecy ends by telling the tragic story of the destruction of Jerusalem. For a Jew, it would be impossible to imagine a scenario more traumatic than this. The city of God is in ruins and the throne of David is empty. The Temple is a pile of rubble and the Ark of the Covenant is missing. The people are in exile in Babylon. The picture Jeremiah paints of these catastrophic events is one of terror and despair. It isn't just the physical pain and material loss that causes God's people to suffer. Far more troubling is the emotional and spiritual trauma of realizing that God has sent wrath and judgment on His people. It seems that God's promises have failed.

> *Zedekiah rebelled against the king of Babylon. And in the ninth year of his reign, in the tenth month, on the tenth day of the month, Nebuchadnezzar king of Babylon came with all his army against Jerusalem, and laid siege to it. And they built siegeworks all around it. So the city was besieged till the eleventh year of King Zedekiah. On the ninth day of the fourth month the famine was so severe in the city that there was no food for the*

9. Max Lucado. *In the Eyes of the Storm* (Dallas: Word Publishing, 1991), 11.

people of the land....Then they captured the king and brought
him up to the king of Babylon at Riblah in the land of Hamath,
and he passed sentence on him. The king of Babylon slaughtered
the sons of Zedekiah before his eyes, and also slaughtered all the
officials of Judah at Riblah. He put out the eyes of Zedekiah,
and bound him in chains, and the king of Babylon took him
to Babylon, and put him in prison till the day of his death. In
the fifth month, on the tenth day of the month...Nebuzaradan
the captain of the bodyguard, who served the king of Babylon,
entered Jerusalem. And he burned the house of the LORD, and
the king's house and all the houses of Jerusalem; every great house
he burned down. And all the army of the Chaldeans, who were
with the captain of the guard, broke down all the walls around
Jerusalem. (Jeremiah 52:3–6, 9–14)

What words can one say in the face of such suffering? Where can
one find comfort? Why did all this happen? What can it possibly
mean? Although the Bible does not try to "solve" all the mysteries
involved in suffering, it does help us to know how to respond when
things fall apart. Jeremiah responds to calamity and adversity by
writing the Book of Lamentations. Because Lamentations is a form
of Hebrew poetry, it is likely intended to be sung. In other words,
Jeremiah responded to suffering by singing the blues.

How Lonely Sits the City

Jeremiah 52 tells us what happened. The Book of Lamentations
tells us how Jeremiah responds to what happened. He doesn't curse,
get drunk, reject God, or seek help from a psychiatrist. He laments.
He pours out his soul in mourning, wailing, and tears to God. He

expresses his grief by singing a lamentation concerning all that has happened. And ever since, this book has been perhaps the most meaningful grief management tool ever written.

The first thing to notice about the Book of Lamentations is that it comprises five poems (songs) corresponding to the five chapters in our English text. Each poem is an acrostic, meaning each stanza of each poem begins with a successive letter of the alphabet. Because the Hebrew alphabet has 22 letters, each chapter has 22 verses, except the third chapter, which has 66 verses (an acrostic with a triple application). As the book progresses we notice some variation in the pattern:

Chapters 1 and 2 have stanzas of three lines each.

Chapter 4 has stanzas of two lines each.

Chapter 5 has stanzas of one line each.

Chapter 3 is different in that each stanza has three verses.

Perhaps the best way to learn how to sing the blues is to survey this short book by walking through it chapter by chapter and listening in as Jeremiah grieves his losses one at a time. Because of space, we can touch only on some of the more poignant verses.

Lamentations 1

How lonely sits the city that was full of people! How like a widow has she become, she who was great among the nations! She who was a princess among the provinces has become a slave. (1:1)

The enemy has stretched out his hands over all her precious things; for she has seen the nations enter her sanctuary, those whom you forbade to enter your congregation. (1:10)

Is it nothing to you, all you who pass by? Look and see if there is any sorrow like my sorrow, which was brought upon me, which the LORD inflicted on the day of his fierce anger. (1:12)

Lamentations 2

The Lord has become like an enemy; he has swallowed up Israel; he has swallowed up all its palaces; he has laid in ruins its strongholds, and he has multiplied in the daughter of Judah mourning and lamentation. (2:5)

My eyes are spent with weeping; my stomach churns; my bile is poured out to the ground because of the destruction of the daughter of my people, because infants and babies faint in the streets of the city. (2:11)

Your prophets have seen for you false and deceptive visions; they have not exposed your iniquity to restore your fortunes, but have seen for you oracles that are false and misleading. (2:14)

All who pass along the way clap their hands at you; they hiss and wag their heads at the daughter of Jerusalem: "Is this the city that was called the perfection of beauty, the joy of all the earth?" (2:15)

Look, O LORD, and see! With whom have you dealt thus? Should women eat the fruit of their womb, the children of their tender care? Should priest and prophet be killed in the sanctuary of the Lord? (2:20)

Lamentations 3

[The Lord] has walled me about so that I cannot escape; he has made my chains heavy; though I call and cry for help, he shuts out my prayer; he has blocked my ways with blocks of stones; he has made my paths crooked. (3:7–9)

[The Lord] is a bear lying in wait for me, a lion in hiding; he turned aside my steps and tore me to pieces; he has made me desolate; he bent his bow and set me as a target for his arrow. (3:10–12)

[The Lord] drove into my kidneys the arrows of his quiver; I have become the laughingstock of all peoples, the object of their taunts all day long. He has filled me with bitterness; he has sated me with wormwood. (3:13–15)

[The Lord] has made my teeth grind on gravel, and made me cower in ashes; my soul is bereft of peace; I have forgotten what happiness is; so I say, "My endurance has perished; so has my hope from the LORD." (3:16–18)

Lamentations 4

The tongue of the nursing infant sticks to the roof of its mouth for thirst; the children beg for food, but no one gives to them. (4:4)

Those who once feasted on delicacies perish in the streets; those who were brought up in purple embrace ash heaps. (4:5)

For the chastisement of the daughter of my people has been greater than the punishment of Sodom, which was overthrown in a moment, and no hands were wrung for her. (4:6)

The hands of compassionate women have boiled their own children; they became their food during the destruction of the daughter of my people. (4:10)

Lamentations 5

Remember, O LORD, what has befallen us; look, and see our disgrace! Our inheritance has been turned over to strangers, our homes to foreigners. We have become orphans, fatherless; our mothers are like widows. (5:1–3)

We have given the hand to Egypt, and to Assyria, to get bread enough. Our fathers sinned, and are no more; and we bear their iniquities. Slaves rule over us; there is none to deliver us from their hand. (5:6–8)

Our skin is hot as an oven with the burning heat of famine. Women are raped in Zion, young women in the towns of Judah. Princes are hung up by their hands; no respect is shown to the elders. (5:10–12)

The joy of our hearts has ceased; our dancing has been turned to mourning. The crown has fallen from our head; woe to us, for we have sinned! (5:15–16)

Why do you forget us forever, why do you forsake us for so many days? Restore us to yourself, O LORD, that we may be restored! Renew our days as of old—unless you have utterly rejected us, and you remain exceedingly angry with us. (5:20–22)

LEARNING TO SING THE BLUES

Jeremiah and his lament over Jerusalem give us a godly model for how *we* should respond to suffering and loss. There is no better grief management tool than this. Here we see the best therapeutic treatment for pain and loss ever devised. When things fall apart, the Book of Lamentations reminds us we must master five skills if we are going to learn how to sing the blues.

Be Real

Don't deny your pain or pretend it doesn't hurt. Don't put on a happy face and force yourself to say, "Praise the Lord!" Unfortunately, many evangelical churches don't allow people the freedom to grieve but push them to a premature claim of joy and victory. Lamentations is written neither to explain your sorrow nor to cure your grief. It is written to help you express them!

It is interesting to note that Buddha is typically portrayed sitting cross-legged under a lotus tree. His eyes are always shut, blocking out the disturbing and painful realities of the world around him. Nirvana comes when those troubling scenes are kept far away at a distance. What a contrast is Jesus, hanging on a cross with his eyes wide open, embracing the pain that is part of this fallen world. Jesus is a real Savior, dealing with real pain in a real world. He did not come to pretend pain and suffering aren't real, but rather to help us know how to face them and find victory through them. If Jesus can be real in the face of tragedy, so can you.

Be Thorough

Lamentations is an acrostic, outlining for those who sing it a sort of alphabet of grief. As the singers work their way systematically through the alphabet, one letter at a time, they can grieve loss after loss after loss. When they have gone through the alphabet of grief once (chapter 1), then they go through it again (chapter 2), then again, and again, and again (chapters 3, 4, 5). In other words, the mourners are being encouraged to grieve everything! Don't leave anything out. Don't look for shortcuts. The way to victory is not to go around grief but *through* it! But after going through the alphabet of grief enough times (perhaps five times through the five chapters), the mourner finally will be ready to say authentically, "I'm done now. With God's help, I'm ready to move on." God's alphabet of abundant living begins when your alphabet of grief ends.

Children's author Dr. Seuss may provide a helpful illustration. In his book *On Beyond Zebra!*[10] we are introduced to a young boy who is learning to spell. Upon learning the 26

> *God's alphabet of abundant living begins when your alphabet of grief ends.*

letters of the alphabet, Conrad Cornelius o'Donald o'Dell assumes he now has all the equipment necessary to comprehend all human knowledge.

> *So now I know everything anyone knows*
> *From beginning to end. From the start to the close.*
> *Because Z is as far as the alphabet goes.*[11]

Conrad's friend, the narrator of the book, then explains to him that there is more to reality than his 26-letter alphabet can account for.

> *Then he almost fell flat on his face on the floor*
> *When I picked up the chalk and drew one letter more!*
> *A letter he never had dreamed of before!*

10. New York: Random House, 1955.
11. Ibid., 3.

And I said, "You can stop, if you want, with the Z
Because most people stop with the Z
But not me!

In the places I go there are things that I see
That I never could spell if I stopped with the Z.
I'm telling you this 'cause you're one of my friends.
My alphabet starts where your alphabet ends! ...[12]

The narrator then begins to introduce young Conrad to letters like YUZZ, WUM, FUDDLE, and GLIKK, which are needed to describe things that could never be experienced if one insists on stopping at Z.

I led him around and I tried hard to show
There are things beyond Z that most people don't know.
I took him past Zebra. As far as I could.
And I think, perhaps, maybe I did him some good...

Because, finally, he said: "This is really great stuff!
And I guess the old alphabet ISN'T enough!"[13]

Jeremiah introduces us to God's alphabet of grace. This alphabet starts where our alphabet ends. When we reach the end of our human abilities, God steps in and introduces us to a world we never even imagined.

Be Connected

Few things are more dangerous and destructive than when someone grieves in isolation, cut off from contact with others. The Book of Lamentations was never meant to be sung alone!

---

12. Ibid., 4–6.
13. Ibid., 45–46.

It is not a solo, but a song meant to be sung in the company of fellow pilgrims. This connection is what makes the Wailing Wall in Jerusalem so powerful. The wall is a public place where people go to grieve—together!

Be Theological

Lamentations is a theological book, not a psychological one. It is about God. As they sing the blues, these grievers are taught to express their sorrow and loss not just to a counselor or to a friend but to God! In his lament, Jeremiah holds God fully responsible for all that has happened. But just as God is the ultimate one responsible for all the pain we feel, so God is also the only one who can truly comfort us and bind up broken hearts.

When we reach the end of our human abilities, God steps in and introduces us to a world we never even imagined.

Be Hopeful

Most of the Book of Lamentations is a woeful recitation of pain and sorrow and loss. But right in the middle of the book is one of the greatest confessions of hope in the entire Bible!

> But this I call to mind,
> and therefore I have hope:
> the steadfast love of the LORD never ceases;
> his mercies never come to an end;
> they are new every morning;
> great is your faithfulness.
> "The LORD is my portion," says my soul,
> "therefore I will hope in him."
> The LORD is good to those who wait for him,
> to the soul who seeks him.

It is good that one should wait quietly
for the salvation of the LORD." (Lamentations 3:21–26)

Regardless how dark the night, how deep the pit, or how intense the pain, God is preparing for His people a future and a hope (Jeremiah 29:11; 31:17).

Questions for Discussion

1. What did God say to you through this lesson?

2. How do most American evangelicals handle grief, suffering, and loss?

3. Does your church permit people to grieve? Why or why not?

4. Does your worship team at church know how to lament and sing the blues?

5. Of the five ways this study encourages you to sing the blues (be real, be thorough, be connected, be theological, and be hopeful), which one is most difficult for you?

6. Can you name an area of pain in your life where you need to learn how to sing the blues?

The Key to Joy

by Stan Key

Broken heart and shattered world,
The center cannot hold;
My faith is feeble, hope is spent,
My love has grown so cold.
It seems, O Lord, that all is lost,
I don't know what to do;
In dark despair, my only cry:
"All I have is You."

And then—a slender ray of hope
Illuminates my tomb;
A tiny spark, the faintest prayer,
Is kindled in the gloom.
I grope for words to help express
What I now see is true;
Into the void I whisper them:
"All I need is You."

The world around me hasn't changed,
The status quo's in place.
But in my heart there's been a shift
For I have seen His face.
And though the old is present yet
I know there's something new;
For now I've found the key to joy:
"All I want is You."